on the cover

Rooney Farm, Mud City, 1998; oil painting by Vermont artist, Rhett Sturman. Characteristically modest, Rhett simply says, "I make paintings." Fortunately, his paintings speak eloquently for themselves. His rich palette serves a perfect accompaniment for the savory, palate-pleasing recipes presented by Vermont Tables in Season. His subject matter, the harvest, captures our agrarian roots and celebrates one of Vermont's rites of summer.

Vermont Tables in Season *began, appropriately enough, around the kitchen table. We were exploring ways to raise money for the school children of Lamoille County. Our criteria: something that would have universal appeal year-round, as well as reflect the unique character of Vermont itself.*

Maybe it was the aroma of the apple pie in the oven or the steaming mugs of hot cider that whetted our appetite for a cookbook. In retrospect, it seems such an obvious solution. After all, Vermont prides itself on its agricultural heritage. From dairy products to maple syrup, Vermont produces some of the finest specialty foods in the world today. Plus, a cookbook answers our most basic need for sustenance. If you are going to take the time to prepare a meal, it might as well be delicious.

The recipes were collected from individuals with a flair for flavor, master chefs, and local restaurants. Without their generous participation and helpful hints, this project would still be simmering on the back burner. From Chocolate Mexican Mousse to Shrimp Mediterranean, authentic Beef Wellington to Indian Cucumber Salad, many of their recipes span the globe. Others, such as Vermont Lamb Triangles and Maple Glazed Walnut Pound Cake, stay closer to home. Whether your culinary tastes are simple or discerning, we promise you'll find some irresistible masterpiece.

As for the title, well, Vermont has its four seasons: summer, fall, winter, and mud. No one is more acutely aware of the seasons than those of us who live in Vermont and whose livelihoods revolve around nature's cycles. Whether tapping maples at winter's end or picking raspberries in summer, Vermont offers an abundance of healthy, natural foods throughout the year.

We've prepared and tasted every recipe. Several pounds later, the results speak for themselves. We hope you enjoy Vermont Tables in Season. *Thank you for your support.*

Linda Post, Kathleen Buchan, Paula Newman, and Lynn Carrell

TABLE OF CONTENTS

SPRING

SUMMER

TABLE OF CONTENTS

AUTUMN

TABLE OF CONTENTS

WINTER

Spring

Maple Spice Muffins

Makes 24 muffins

Ingredients

- 1 cup whole wheat flour
- 1 cup all-purpose flour
- $\frac{1}{2}$ cup rolled oats
- $\frac{3}{4}$ cup bran
- 2 teaspoon baking powder
- 1 teaspoon baking soda
- 2 teaspoon ground cinnamon
- $\frac{1}{2}$ teaspoon ground cloves
- 2 eggs, beaten
- 1 8-ounce container of plain yogurt
- 1 cup maple syrup
- $\frac{1}{2}$ cup brown sugar
- $\frac{1}{2}$ cup cooking oil
- 1 cup walnuts, chopped
- 1 cup mashed ripe bananas (two bananas)

Directions

1. Preheat oven to 400°.
2. Stir together flours, oats, bran, powder, soda, and spices.
3. Combine eggs, yogurt, and syrup.
4. Beat in brown sugar and oil.
5. Add dry ingredients, nuts, and bananas.
6. Stir until mixed.
7. Spoon into greased or baking paper cup-lined muffin pans; 2/3 full.
8. Bake in 400° oven, 15 to 20 minutes.
9. Optional: Drizzle additional syrup on top while warm.

Crêpes

Serves 4

Ingredients

3 whole eggs

$1\frac{1}{2}$ cup milk

$\frac{7}{8}$ cup flour

scant $\frac{1}{4}$ cup oil (combination canola and orange oils)

1 teaspoon sugar

$\frac{1}{2}$ teaspoon salt

Optional $\frac{1}{2}$ teaspoon grated orange zest

Clarified butter for cooking the crepes

Filling suggestions

1. Mix fresh strawberries with lightly sweetened whipped cream, and garnish with dollop of whipped cream.

2. Any fresh fruit, cut to bite-size pieces.

3. Omit sugar in batter and use savory filling such as crabmeat and asparagus with a little Hollandaise sauce.

Directions

1. Place all ingredients except clarified butter in blender.

2. Blend on medium/high speed for 1 minute.

3. Refrigerate for at least 1/2 hour.

4. Heat crêpe pan (or any small, heavy-bottomed sauté pan with smooth surface) to moderately high.

5. Coat pan with clarified butter.

6. Pour in 1 1/2 tablespoons batter and swirl around to create thin, even coating.

7. Cook approximately 1 minute each side, adjusting time and temperature as necessary until lightly browned and lacey.

8. Stack crêpes as they are cooked.

9. Put dollop of filling in center.

10. Roll crêpe or fold into cornet shape.

Omelette

Serves 4

Ingredients

8 eggs

4 tablespoons milk or half-and-half

1 teaspoon salt

Freshly ground pepper to taste

Directions

1. Whisk eggs together.

2. Add milk, salt, and pepper.

3. Pour into lightly greased omelette pan and swirl around.

4. When almost set, add filling ingredients.

5. Flip and cook until set, being careful not to burn.

Filling Options

1. Add 2 tablespoons chopped fresh cilantro to egg mixture. Fill with chopped avocado, grated cheddar cheese, and salsa to taste.

2. Cream cheese cut into small squares, chopped sundried tomatoes, and chopped arugula to taste.

3. Add 2 tablespoons fresh oregano to egg mixture. Fill with fresh chopped spinach, pitted, chopped Kalamata olives, fresh tomatoes, and crumbled feta cheese to taste.

Breakfast Burrito with Spinach

Serves 4

Ingredients

4 Spinach flour tortillas (or chili tortillas), warmed

6 eggs, room temperature beaten with 2 tablespoons light cream

2 ounces of your favorite cheese, grated

1 small onion, diced and sautéed in a little butter

2 cups fresh spinach, chopped

$\frac{1}{3}$ cup leaves of fresh sweet basil, chopped

4 teaspoons butter

Salt and pepper to taste

8 tablespoons of your favorite salsa (optional)

Directions

1. Heat 1 teaspoon of butter on high heat until sizzling.

2. Whisk eggs, seasoning with salt and pepper to taste and pour into pan.

3. Fold in the spinach, basil, onion, and cheese after the eggs have set.

4. Place the warmed tortilla on a work surface and spoon the eggs onto the tortilla.

5. Spoon the salsa over the eggs and roll the tortilla.

6. Serve with sour cream and extra salsa if desired.

Strawberry French Toast

Serves 6

Ingredients

6 eggs

1$\frac{1}{2}$ cup half-and-half

12 slices bread

$\frac{1}{2}$ cup butter, softened

$\frac{1}{3}$ cup plus 6 tablespoons strawberry preserves

Fresh strawberry slices

Powdered sugar

Toasted almonds

Directions

1. Beat eggs and 6 tablespoons strawberry preserves to blend.

2. Add half-and-half.

3. Place single layer of bread in pan and pour mixture over bread.

4. Cover and refrigerate overnight until most of liquid is absorbed.

5. Beat 1/3 cup strawberry preserves and 4 tablespoons butter until fluffy; set aside.

6. Melt 2 tablespoons butter in skillet, add bread, and cook until brown.

7. Remove and keep warm.

8. Top with strawberry butter and fresh strawberries and sprinkle with almonds and sugar.

Vermont Lamb Triangles

Makes 2 dozen

Ingredients

Filling

- $\frac{1}{4}$ cup bulgur
- 1 cup hot water
- $\frac{1}{2}$ pound lean ground lamb
- 1 teaspoon olive oil
- $\frac{1}{3}$ cup onion, finely chopped
- 1 clove garlic, minced
- $\frac{1}{3}$ cup reduced-sodium chicken broth, defatted
- 2 tablespoons golden raisins, chopped
- 2 tablespoons fresh mint, chopped
- 1 tablespoon fresh lemon juice
- 1 tablespoon tomato paste
- $\frac{1}{2}$ teaspoon salt
- $\frac{1}{4}$ teaspoon freshly ground black pepper
- $\frac{1}{4}$ teaspoon freshly grated nutmeg
- $\frac{1}{4}$ teaspoon ground cinnamon

Pastry

- 3 tablespoons olive oil
- 12 sheets phyllo dough, thawed
- $1\frac{1}{2}$ teaspoons sesame seeds

Directions

Filling

1. Combine bulgur and water in bowl, set aside to soften, about 30 minutes.

2. Drain and set aside.

3. Cook lamb in large non-stick skillet over medium-high heat, breaking up into small pieces with wooden spoon, until well-browned, approximately 3 to 5 minutes.

4. Transfer to paper-towel-lined plate to drain; wipe out skillet.

5. Heat oil in skillet over low heat.

6. Add onion and garlic and cook, stirring, until onion is soft and golden, about 5 to 7 minutes (add 1 tablespoon of water if onions get too dry).

7. Add lamb, reserved bulgur, chicken broth, raisins, mint, lemon juice, tomato paste, salt, pepper, nutmeg, and cinnamon; return to simmer.

8. Cook, stirring often, until liquid has been absorbed, approximately 5 to 10 minutes.

9. Adjust seasonings and cool.

Pastry

1. Preheat oven to 375°.

2. Lightly oil a baking sheet.

3. Put oil in small bowl and dampen pastry brush.

4. Lay 1 sheet of phyllo on work surface with a short side closest to you.

5. Brush lightly with oil and place another sheet of phyllo on top.

6. Lightly brush with more oil and cut lengthwise into 4 strips.

7. Place 1 tablespoon of filling at the bottom of each strip and fold one corner of the strip diagonally over the filling to the opposite edge, forming a triangle.

8. Continue folding the filling up in the pastry, as you would a flag.

9. Place on prepared baking sheet.

10. Repeat with remaining phyllo and filling to form 24 triangles.

11. Brush tops lightly with oil and sprinkle with sesame seeds.

12. Bake for 15 to 20 minutes, or until golden brown and crisp.

13. Cool slightly before serving.

Note: Triangles can be formed, then frozen on a baking sheet, and later transferred to plastic storage bags. They will keep, frozen, for up to 1 month. Do not thaw before baking.

Skewered Sesame Chicken with Chili Dip

Serves 12

Ingredients

- 2 tablespoons rice wine vinegar
- 2 tablespoons dark sesame oil
- 1 tablespoon chopped fresh garlic
- 2 tablespoons soy sauce
- $1\frac{1}{3}$ pounds boneless chicken breasts
- $\frac{1}{4}$ cup white sesame seeds
- $\frac{1}{4}$ cup dark sesame seeds
- 2 teaspoons cornstarch
- 3 tablespoons flour
- Peanut oil
- 48 snow peas

Chili Sauce

- 1 tablespoon rice wine vinegar
- 2 tablespoons chili paste with garlic (if you use plain chili paste, add 1 glove of garlic)
- 1 tablespoon soy sauce
- 1 teaspoon sesame oil
- 1 tablespoon fresh ginger, minced
- $\frac{3}{4}$ cup mayonnaise
- 1 tablespoon sugar
- Dash Tabasco

Directions

1. Cut chicken into 48 bite-size pieces.
2. Mix vinegar, sesame oil, garlic, and soy sauce and pour over chicken.
3. Cover and refrigerate overnight.
4. Combine sesame seeds, cornstarch, and flour; dip chicken pieces into the mixture.
5. Let stand for 10 minutes.
6. Heat peanut oil in sauté pan and brown chicken, in batches, on all sides.
7. Drain on paper towels.
8. Remove tips, tails, and strings from snow peas.
9. Steam over boiling water, covered, for 1 minute.
10. Immerse in ice water, then pat dry.
11. Wrap each pea pod around a piece of chicken and secure with wooden skewer; serve with Chili sauce.

Chili Sauce Directions:

Mix all ingredients together.

Spring Lamb Chops with Roasted Pepper Goat Cheese Crema

Serves 4

Ingredients

- 2 each $\frac{1}{2}$ racks of Colorado lamb - Frenched
- 2 tablespoons rosemary
- 1 large bunch watercress
- 1 head Belgian endive
- $\frac{1}{4}$ cup rice vinegar
- 4 tablespoons olive oil
- $\frac{1}{2}$ tablespoon honey
- 1 red pepper
- $\frac{1}{2}$ cup sour cream
- 1 ounce goat cheese
- 1 tablespoon water
- Salt and fresh cracked pepper to taste

Directions

1. Use 1 teaspoon olive oil to coat pepper and fire-roast on grill or under broiler.

2. Peel pepper and remove seeds, reserve.

3. Purée pepper, goat cheese, and sour cream in blender or food processor until smooth. Season with salt and pepper as needed.

4. Clean watercress by saving top three inches of each sprig. Slice endive in half and remove core, slice into thin strips and combine with watercress. Set aside.

5. Slice lamb racks into 8 chops and coat with 2 teaspoons olive oil, then dust with chopped rosemary. Set aside.

6. In a small mixing bowl, whisk rice vinegar, warm honey, and 2 tablespoons oil together until well incorporated. Adjust seasoning.

7. Toss watercress/endive with rice vinegar dressing and make 4 equal portions on appetizer plates.

8. Season lamb chops with salt and pepper. Then in hot sauté pan, add remaining oil and sear chops until rare/medium-rare. Arrange on plate so bones are criss-crossing and garnish with crema.

Smoked Salmon Cheesecake

Serves 16

Ingredients

- $\frac{1}{2}$ cup fine, dry bread crumbs
- 1 12-ounce (1 large) onion, chopped
- 3 tablespoons butter
- 3 eight-ounce packages cream cheese at room temperature
- 8 ounces smoked salmon, chopped
- 4 eggs
- 2 tablespoons lemon juice
- 2 tablespoons minced fresh dill ($\frac{3}{4}$ teaspoon dried)

Garnish

Fresh dill sprigs

Thin slices lemon

Strips of smoked salmon

Directions

1. Preheat oven to 325°.

2. Sprinkle bread crumbs onto bottom and halfway up sides of a greased 8-inch spring-form pan.

3. Cook onion in butter in small skillet over medium heat for 5 minutes or until tender and remove from heat.

4. Process cream cheese in food processor until smooth.

5. Add chopped salmon, cooked onion, eggs, lemon juice, dill and process until completely smooth.

6. Pour into prepared pan.

7. Place pan in larger, deeper, baking pan; pour hot water in outer pan to come halfway up the sides of inner pan.

8. Bake for 1 hour.

9. Turn off oven \and cool cheesecake in oven, with door slightly ajar, for 1 hour.

10. Remove pan from water and cool completely before refrigerating.

11. To serve, remove carefully from pan, garnish, and serve at room temperature.

Maple Sweet-and-Sour Dressing

Ingredients

$\frac{1}{2}$ cup oil

$\frac{1}{2}$ cup vinegar

$\frac{1}{2}$ cup catsup

$\frac{3}{4}$–1 cup maple syrup

$\frac{1}{2}$ teaspoon horseradish

1 teaspoon garlic, minced

Directions

1. Mix all ingredients together thoroughly.

2. Toss with mixed greens.

Wilted Spinach Salad with Hot Bacon Dressing

Serves 4

Ingredients

- $\frac{1}{2}$ pound bacon, diced
- $\frac{1}{2}$ cup onion, diced
- 1 cup cider vinegar
- 1 cup oil
- 1 cup water
- 1 tablespoon cornstarch, dissolved in the water
- $\frac{1}{2}$ cup honey
- 1 teaspoon salt
- 1 teaspoon coarse ground pepper
- 2 pounds spinach, washed
- 2 hard-boiled eggs, quartered
- 4 radishes, sliced

Directions

1. Fry the bacon in a two-quart casserole until crisp. Reserve the bacon.

2. Sauté the onions in the bacon fat. Don't allow them to brown.

3. Deglaze with vinegar and oil. Bring to a simmer.

4. Add the water with the dissolved cornstarch in it and simmer for a few minutes.

5. Add the honey, salt, and pepper.

6. To assemble the salad, pour 1 cup of the liquid dressing in a large frying pan. Add the clean spinach and wilt.

7. Place in a glass salad bowl. Sprinkle with bacon. Garnish with eggs and radish slices.

Kalamata Olive Dressing

Serves 4 to 6

Ingredients

1 cup extra virgin olive oil

$\frac{1}{4}$ cup balsamic vinegar

$\frac{1}{2}$ cup pitted kalamata olives

$\frac{1}{2}$ cup fresh finely crumbled feta cheese

Cracked black pepper to taste

Directions

1. In a blender, puree first 3 ingredients

2. Stir in the feta cheese and black pepper to taste.

Serve over your favorite greens.

Spinach Salad with Lemon Soy Dressing

Serves 4

Ingredients

- 1 pound fresh spinach [not baby] cleaned and stems removed

  Mandarin oranges, canned

- $\frac{1}{4}$ cup chopped walnuts

Dressing

- $\frac{1}{4}$ cup canola oil

- 2 tablespoons fresh lemon juice

- 2 tablespoons soy sauce

- 1 tablespoon orange juice

- $\frac{1}{2}$ clove garlic, minced

Directions

1. Mix all dressing ingredients, and let stand for 1 hour.

2. So as not to have pieces of garlic in your dressing, strain before serving.

3. Pour sparingly over spinach and toss.

4. Add Mandarin oranges and walnuts, then serve.

Spring Parsnip Bisque with Cheddar Cheese Crisps

Serves 4

The best parsnips are wintered over in the ground and dug up in the spring when the ground thaws. Hopefully your farmer will get them out of the ground before the deer do.

Ingredients

2 pounds parsnips

4 medium onions

1 medium potato

4 tablespoons olive oil (reserve 2 for garnish)

1$\frac{1}{2}$ quarts chicken or vegetable broth

Salt and white pepper

4 thin slices day-old French bread

Handful of grated sharp cheddar cheese

Italian parsley, coarsely chopped for garnish

Directions

1. Peel and chop parsnips, onions, and potato.

2. In a large, heavy pot, sauté the parsnips and onions in 2 tablespoons olive oil, very slowly until they release their juices.

3. Add the potato, 1/2 teaspoon salt, and stock; simmer until potato is very soft.

4. Carefully, using a quick pulse, purée everything in a blender until very smooth.

5. Check seasoning, adding white pepper judiciously.

6. Meanwhile, coat the French bread with olive oil and bake in moderate oven until golden and crisp.

7. When ready to serve, just reheat soup.

8. Melt the cheese on the croutons and set on the soup with the parsley just before serving.

Potato Leek Soup

Serves 8 to 10

Ingredients

- 4 slices bacon, cut into 1-inch pieces
- $\frac{1}{2}$ stick butter
- 2 cups finely diced leeks
- $1\frac{1}{2}$ cups finely diced onions
- 1 cup finely diced celery
- $1\frac{3}{4}$ teaspoons dried tarragon
- $\frac{1}{2}$ teaspoon dried thyme
- $\frac{1}{4}$ teaspoon salt
- $\frac{1}{8}$ teaspoon white pepper
- 5 cups chicken stock
- 2 to 3 cups finely diced potatoes
- $\frac{1}{2}$ cup heavy cream

Directions

1. Cook bacon over low heat until fat is rendered.

2. Remove bacon and discard.

3. Add butter to pot and melt.

4. Add leeks, onions, and celery and cook over low heat until wilted.

5. Add tarragon, thyme, salt, and pepper and stir well.

6. Add the stock and potatoes; cover and simmer until potatoes are tender but not mushy.

7. Remove the soup from heat; purée half of the soup in a food processor and return the purée to the soup pot.

8. Add the cream and heat through, stirring well, but do not boil.

Spring Minestrone

Serves 6

Ingredients

3 celery ribs, finely chopped

1 large red onion, peeled and chopped

3 cloves of garlic, minced

4 tablespoons olive oil

2 pounds young, fresh asparagus, cut into 1-inch pieces (use only tender parts, set tips aside)

$\frac{1}{2}$ pound fresh green beans, cut into 1-inch pieces

1 pound fresh peas

1 pound shelled fava beans, blanched and peeled

4 cups chicken stock

$\frac{1}{4}$ cup fresh basil, finely chopped

1 cup heavy cream

$\frac{1}{2}$ cup pesto

1 cup Parmesan cheese, grated

Salt and pepper to taste

Directions

1. In a heavy saucepan, sauté the celery, garlic, and onions in olive oil until soft.

2. Add all remaining vegetables, except asparagus tips and sauté for 10 minutes, stirring occasionally.

3. Season with salt and pepper to taste.

4. Add the chicken stock and bring to a boil.

5. Reduce heat and simmer for 30 minutes.

6. Add asparagus tips and cook for another 10 minutes.

7. Remove from heat and gently stir in the pesto, basil, cream, and cheese.

Vegetable Strudel

Serves 6

Ingredients

- 1 carrot, julienne
- 1 red pepper, julienne
- 1 medium onion, diced
- $\frac{1}{2}$ pound fresh spinach
- 3 tablespoons butter
- 1 teaspoon salt
- $\frac{1}{4}$ teaspoon pepper
- $\frac{1}{4}$ teaspoon thyme
- 2 cups pinto or kidney beans, drained
- 1 cup Monterey Jack cheese, grated
- 6 sheets Phyllo dough
- 2 tablespoons bread crumbs
- Paprika

Directions

1. Preheat oven to 375°.
2. Sauté vegetables in 1 tablespoon butter until crisp and tender. Remove from heat.
3. Add spices, beans, and cheese.
4. Melt 2 tablespoons butter.
5. Place 1 sheet of Phyllo dough on work surface.
6. Brush with butter and sprinkle with crumbs.
7. Continue layering all sheets.
8. On last sheets spoon mixture along one long edge two inches from edge.
9. Roll up, tucking in sides, and place seam down on greased baking sheet.
10. Brush with butter and sprinkle with paprika.
11. Make slashes on the top of strudel about 2 inches apart. When serving, slice where the slashes were made.
12. Bake at 375° for 25 minutes.

Serve as an entrée.

Gougère with Asparagus

Serves 6 to 8

Ingredients

1 cup water

$\frac{1}{4}$ pound butter

$\frac{1}{2}$ teaspoon salt

1 cup all-purpose unbleached flour

4 eggs

$\frac{1}{4}$ pound diced Gruyère

$1\frac{1}{2}$ pounds asparagus spears, peeled, blanched and cut into 1-inch pieces

1 large, yellow spanish onion, sliced

1 tablespoon fresh, chopped rosemary

$\frac{1}{2}$ cup Fontina, grated

Directions

1. Bring water to a boil with butter and salt.

2. Add the flour all at once.

3. Turn off the heat and stir vigorously until the dough comes away from the sides of the pan.

4. Transfer the mixture to the Kitchen Aid Mixer, and with the paddle attachment and the mixer running at low speed, add the eggs, one at a time, beating only until each egg is incorporated before adding the next

one. Try to be quick and efficient in this step.

5. Return the dough to the pan on the stove over low heat; stir and flip until batter is shiny and smooth.

6. Add the diced Gruyère and incorporate thoroughly.

7. Chill one hour.

8. Preheat oven to 400°.

9. While the dough (Pâté à Choux) is chilling, prepare the asparagus by blanching for 1 minute; carmelize the onions and grate the Fontina (as best you can).

10. Spray a 9x12-inch baking pan with vegalene, then spread a thin layer of the Pâté à Choux dough on the bottom and sides.

11. Bake at 400° until puffed, golden brown, and completely done about—15 to 20 minutes.

12. Making sure the blanched asparagus is completely dry and the onions are caramelized (or cooked to your specifications), top the Gougère with the asparagus, onions, and Fontina and pop back into a 450° oven for a few minutes until the garnish is hot and the cheese is bubbly and brown, (should take 5 to 10 minutes).

13. Serve uncovered so the pastry doesn't become soggy.

Vidalia Onion Stuffed with Bud's Sausage

Serves 4

Ingredients

4 large Vidalia onions

Olive oil

Salt and pepper

1 pound Bud's sausage*

Handful fresh bread crumbs

$\frac{1}{2}$ teaspoon fresh chopped thyme

1 tablespoon fresh chopped Italian parsley

Handful fresh grated Parmesan or Sardo cheese

*Bud's sausage is a great sausage from Howard's Friendly Market in South Barre, Vermont. If you can't get Bud's, use your favorite Italian sausage.

Directions

1. Preheat oven to 375°.

2. Peel the onion, trimming the root so onion can just stand up but without cutting off too much. Leave the stem in-tact as much as possible.

3. Rub each onion with oil, salt, and pepper. Place in roasting dish, cover tightly with foil, and roast in a moderate oven until tender, about 40 minutes—check with a paring knife; the onion should be soft. Take care not to let it overcook or it will fall apart. Allow to cool.

4. Meanwhile, remove Bud's sausage from its casing and sauté until fully cooked. By this time the sausage should be in small pieces. If not, roughly chop.

5. Once the onion is cool, cut off the stem end, then with a paring knife and spoon, hollow out the onion (saving the scraps) without disturbing the outer layers of the onion.

6. Chop the onion scraps and mix them with the sausage. Add the herbs and bread crumbs. Mix, then fill the hollows of each onion with the stuffing.

7. Cover the top with cheese and bake until the cheese is golden and crispy.

Grilled Sunshine Lamb Chops

Serves 8

Ingredients

8 lamb chops

$\frac{1}{2}$ cup honey

$\frac{1}{2}$ cup Dijon-style mustard

Salt and pepper to taste

Directions

1. Mix honey, mustard, salt, and pepper.

2. Brush glaze on lamb chops and grill 3 inches from heat for approximately 7 minutes, depending on thickness of chops.

3. Turn chops, grill until done, approximately 7 minutes more, brushing with remaining glaze while cooking.

Suggested Wine

Rich Merlot
Red Zinfandel

Chicken with Artichoke Hearts

Serves 4

Ingredients

4 six-ounce, dry, skinless chicken breasts

$1\frac{1}{2}$ cups medium shallots, peeled

1 can artichoke hearts, drained, rinsed and halved

1 18-ounce chicken stock or broth

$\frac{1}{2}$ cup Chardonnay wine

2 ounces fresh lemon juice

1 teaspoon chopped parsley

3 ounces cold, unsalted butter, cut into small chunks

$1\frac{1}{2}$ ounces clarified butter

1 lemon, cut into thin rings

$\frac{1}{4}$ teaspoon salt

$\frac{1}{8}$ teaspoon fresh ground pepper

Directions

1. Braise shallots in 4 ounces of chicken stock for five minutes in small sauce pan.

Suggested Wine

Chardonnay

2. Strain and set aside.

3. In a 10-inch sauté pan, heat clarified butter until almost smoking; place chicken breasts in the pan

4. Cook chicken at medium heat uncovered for 3 to 4 minutes or until skin side is golden brown.

5. Turn breasts, cover, turn heat down low and let cook for about 4 minutes (or place in a 425° oven for 6 to 7 minutes, uncovered).

6. Add 12 ounces of stock to pan and reduce by 1/3.

7. Add shallots, artichokes, and lemon juice to reduced stock and cook for 3 minutes, stirring gently.

8. While sauce is reducing, remove shallots and artichokes with a slotted spoon and arrange around chicken breasts.

9. Strain sauce through a small sieve into a small saucepan and bring to boil.

10. Turn off heat; swirl in unsalted butter with a whisk.

11. Season with salt and pepper to taste.

12. Ring plate with lemons, spoon sauce, shallots, and artichokes over chicken.

13. Garnish with chopped parsley.

Fresh Pasta with Morels, Ramps*
and English Garden Peas

Serves 4

Ingredients

1 pound fresh fettucine

$\frac{1}{2}$ pound fresh morels

16 ramps cleaned, greens removed and set aside (if available)

1 pound English garden peas in pods

1 cup white wine

1 cup crème fraiche (fresh cream)

Salt and pepper to taste

Oil for sauté

Fresh chervil for garnish (can substitute chives)

Directions

1. Clean morels with a cloth, rinse only if they appear to be gritty.

2. In a heated sauté pan, add oil then the white parts of the ramps and morels. Sauté for a minute and add the wine. Lower heat and simmer for 10 minutes letting wine reduce by half.

3. Bring a large pot of water to boil. Shell the peas and add them to the boiling water. Cook until just tender.

4. Using a strainer, fish peas from the water and leave the water to boil.

5. Set aside the peas and reheat the mushroom mix. Add the crème fraiche; heat the mixture until it starts to bubble. Season to taste.

6. Cook the pasta in the boiling water (will only take a minute or two). Drain and toss with a little oil to prevent sticking.

7. Place pasta in a large pasta bowl and pour the mushrooms over the middle of the pasta; garnish and serve.

*Ramps are also known as wild leeks and wild garlic. You can find them at farmers' markets and natural food markets in the spring.

Suggested Wine
━━◆━━
Dry Gewürztraminer
Spanish Rioja
Sangiovese

Maple-Soy Broiled Salmon with Cucumber Salad

Serves 4

Ingredients

4 7-ounce filets of Atlantic salmon

Marinade

$\frac{1}{2}$ cup light soy sauce

$\frac{1}{3}$ cup maple syrup

1 cup apple cider

1 ounce ginger root, crushed

3 cloves garlic, minced

1 bay leaf

6 black peppercorns

$\frac{1}{4}$ cup butter

Salad

2 medium cucumbers, halved lengthwise, seeded and thinly sliced

1 small carrot, thinly sliced into three-inch strips

1 small red bell pepper, thinly sliced into strips

$\frac{1}{2}$ cup thinly sliced red onion

$\frac{1}{2}$ teaspoon grated fresh ginger

$\frac{1}{2}$ teaspoon minced garlic

1 tablespoon chopped cilantro

1 teaspoon toasted sesame seeds

2 tablespoons vegetable oil

2 teaspoons rice wine vinegar

1 tablespoon sugar

Juice and zest of one lime

$\frac{1}{4}$ teaspoon salt

$\frac{1}{8}$ teaspoon pepper

Directions

1. Combine ingredients for cucumber salad. Toss well and refrigerate for several hours.

2. Combine all ingredients for marinade in a medium saucepan and reduce liquid by half on medium heat.

3. Place the salmon filets in a shallow baking tray and spoon a liberal amount of marinade over them. Let sit for one hour.

4. Bake the salmon for 6 to 8 minutes in an oven preheated to 375°, then broil for 2 minutes or until sauce is lightly caramelized.

5. Serve with cucumber salad draped diagonally across the salmon.

Suggested Wine

Rich Riesling
Dry or Slightly off-dry Gewürztraminer
Beaujolais
California Pinot Noir

Grilled Tenderloin of Beef with a Mustard-Mint Sauce

Serves 8

Ingredients

1 whole beef tenderloin
(4-5 pounds)

Olive oil

Freshly ground black pepper

Sauce

1 egg yolk

1 tablespoon Dijon mustard

1 tablespoon grainy mustard

1 tablespoon white wine vinegar

$\frac{1}{2}$ teaspoon salt

freshly ground pepper to taste

$\frac{3}{4}$ cup olive oil

1 tablespoon heavy cream

$\frac{1}{2}$ teaspoon sugar

2-3 tablespoons chopped fresh mint leaves

Directions

1. Prepare sauce. Combine egg yolk, mustards, vinegar, salt, and pepper in a blender or food processor.

2. Add the oil, in a thin stream, with the blender or food processor running until the mixture thickens.

3. Transfer the sauce to a bowl and whisk in cream and sugar.

4. Stir in fresh mint leaves.

5. Set sauce aside until ready to serve.

6. Prepare tenderloin. Bring tenderloin to room temperature before grilling.

7. Brush generously with olive oil and season with pepper to taste.

8. Oil the cooking rack as well.

9. On an open grill over red-hot coals, sear the tenderloin for 2 minutes on both sides to seal in juices.

10. Cover the grill, but leave vents partially open. Cook the tenderloin for approximately 10 minutes per side for rare (until a meat thermometer registers 120°F); approximately 12 minutes per side for medium-rare (130°F); or approximately 15 minutes per side for medium-well done (145°F).

11. Slice meat into 3/4-inch slices and serve with mustard-mint sauce.

12. Tenderloin can also be roasted in the oven. Preheat oven to 475°. Place in buttered roasting pan; roast uncovered, turning once, for about 25 minutes for medium-rare.

Suggested Wine

California Cabernet, especially one with hints of Eucalyptus or Anise

Chicken with Soy and Ginger Glaze

Serves 6

Ingredients

6 chicken breasts, skinned, boned, halved

$\frac{1}{2}$ cup Japanese soy sauce or Tamari

$\frac{1}{2}$ cup sherry

2 cups water

2 cloves garlic, crushed

2-3 slices fresh ginger root

2 tablespoons sugar

Directions

1. Combine all ingredients except chicken in a large saucepan and bring to a boil.

2. Add chicken and simmer, covered, for approximately 20 minutes.

3. Cool, then refrigerate 4 hours or overnight.

4. Grill, or broil until brown and crispy.

Can make with shrimp instead of chicken.

Suggested Wine

Riesling
Pinot Gris (Grigio)

Vegetarian Loaf

Serves 4 to 6

Ingredients

- 1 cup almonds
- 1 cup walnuts
- $\frac{1}{2}$ cup sunflower seeds
- 1 onion, finely chopped
- 2 stalks celery, chopped
- 2 cloves garlic, chopped
- 2 cups large curd cottage cheese
- 2 cups brown rice
- 2 eggs, beaten
- $\frac{1}{2}$ cup chopped parsley
- 1 teaspoon caraway seeds (optional)

Suggestions

Feel free to improvise with your choice of nuts. Raw cashews work equally well.

Serve with poached eggs and homemade catsup or salsa.

Directions

Brown Rice

1. Bring 1 1/3 cups water to a rolling boil.
2. Add 1/4 teaspoon salt and 1 teaspoon butter
3. Slowly stir 1/2 cup rice into water.
4. Cover and cook over slow heat, 40 to 50 minutes.

For Loaf

1. Preheat oven to 350°.
2. Chop nuts in Cuisinart until they resemble a coarse meal.
3. Combine all ingredients until well blended.
4. Spoon into a shallow baking dish or loaf pan.
5. Bake at 350° for 1 hour until lightly crusted.

Shrimp Mediterranean

Serves 4

Ingredients

24 medium shrimp

2 tablespoons olive oil

1½ teaspoons minced shallots

1½ teaspoons minced garlic

16 artichoke hearts, quartered

½ cup roasted red pepper, cut in thin strips

¼ cup sundried tomatoes cut in thin strips

16 kalamata olives, cut in half and pitted

½ cup white wine

2 tablespoons lemon juice

2 teaspoons prepared lobster base

¼ teaspoon salt

⅛ teaspoon pepper

1½ teaspoons butter

½ pound fettuccine

Fresh parsley for garnish

Directions

1. Shell and devein shrimp.

2. Heat olive oil in pan; cook shrimp until just pink on each side and set aside.

3. Sauté garlic and shallots in the oil under low heat until fragrant.

4. Add artichoke hearts, roasted red pepper, sundried tomatoes, and olives and continue to sauté until heated through.

5. Deglaze pan with white wine and lemon juice, add lobster base and reduce liquids by half.

6. Add butter and return shrimp to the pan, by the time the butter is incorporated the shrimp will be fully cooked.

Serve over fettuccine and garnish with chopped parsley.

Suggested Wine

Loire White
Sancerre or Pouilly Fumé
American Sauvignon Blanc

Chicken Alfredo

Serves 6

Ingredients

- $\frac{3}{4}$ pound angel hair pasta
- $1\frac{1}{4}$ pounds chicken breasts, cut in strips
- 1 tablespoon olive oil
- $\frac{1}{3}$ pound Shitake mushrooms with stems removed, julienne
- 2 leeks, whites only, julienne
- $\frac{1}{2}$ tablespoon fresh garlic
- $1\frac{1}{4}$ cups heavy cream
- $\frac{1}{3}$ cup white wine
- 3 ounces fresh parmesan cheese
- $\frac{1}{2}$ teaspoon salt
- $\frac{1}{4}$ teaspoon pepper

Directions

1. Cook angel hair pasta; don't rinse; season with salt, pepper, garlic, and olive oil.

2. Sauté chicken strips; remove and hold in 1 tablespoon olive oil.

3. Sauté mushrooms, leeks, and garlic.

4. Add white wine and reduce to 1/2.

5. Return chicken.

6. Add pasta, cream, and parmesan cheese.

7. Adjust seasoning.

Suggested Wine

Rich Chardonnay

Burnt Almond Parfait

Serves 6

Ingredients

$\frac{1}{2}$ cup sugar

$\frac{1}{2}$ cup boiling water

2 teaspoons unflavored gelatin

1 tablespoon cold water

$1\frac{1}{2}$ cups heavy cream

$\frac{1}{4}$ cup blanched almonds

1 teaspoon vanilla extract

Directions

1. Pour 1/4 cup of sugar into a saucepan and cook over medium heat stirring constantly, until sugar turns a rich caramel color. Then take it off the range and cool for 1 to 2 minutes.

2. At this point, add the boiling water and cook over a low heat for several minutes until hardened syrup has remelted into water.

3. Sprinkle gelatin over cold water to soften. When soft, stir gelatin and 1/2 cup cream into syrup and cool in refrigerator until thick and heavy cream (about 10 to 20 minutes).

4. Beat remaining cream with remaining sugar and vanilla extract until stiff.

5. Mix gently or fold into the thickened syrup mixture. If your syrup mixture has set and you are unable to fold the whipped cream into it, you can blend in a blender until smooth. Freeze in stainless steel bowl until mushy.

6. Preheat oven to 400°.

7. Place almonds in a pie pan and toast in oven until rich deep brown in color.

8. Chop nuts rather coarsely.

9. When parfait reaches mushy stage, stir in chopped almonds and beat several minutes.

10. Pour into freezing tray or mold and freeze about 3 1/2 hours until firm.

For those who need not consider dieting!

This can be made a day in advance, then removed from the freezer and refrigerated several hours before serving.

Maple Rice Pudding

Serves 6

Ingredients

- 3 eggs
- 1 cup Vermont maple syrup
- 2 cups milk
- 2 cups boiled rice
- $\frac{1}{2}$ teaspoon salt (optional)
- $\frac{1}{2}$ teaspoon nutmeg
- 1 cup raisins

Directions

1. Preheat oven to 350°.
2. Butter baking dish.
3. Beat eggs slightly.
4. Add syrup, milk, rice, salt, nutmeg, and raisins.
5. Bake approximately 45 minutes until firm.

Key Lime Pie

Serves 8

Ingredients

1 9-inch graham cracker pie crust, preferably homemade

1 can sweetened condensed milk

4 egg yolks

5 ounces lime juice

Directions

1. Bake crust at 350° for 8 to 10 minutes

2. Mix condensed milk and egg yolks. Add lime juice. Mix well.

3. Pour into pie crust. Bake 8 to 10 minutes more.

4. Remove from oven. Cool.

5. Garnish with slightly sweetened whipped cream and thin slices of lime.

Strawberries with Grand Marnier

Serves 6

Ingredients

3 pints strawberries, cleaned and halved

$\frac{1}{4}$ cup superfine sugar

$\frac{1}{4}$ cup Grand Marnier or Cointreau

$\frac{1}{2}$ teaspoon grated orange peel

Whipped cream or frozen yogurt

Directions:

1. Toss first four items together and refrigerate for a few hours.

2. Serve with whipped cream or frozen yogurt.

Maple Pecan Pie

Serves 8

Ingredients

- $\frac{1}{4}$ cup butter
- $\frac{1}{2}$ cup Vermont maple sugar (or granulated sugar)
- $\frac{1}{2}$ teaspoon salt (optional)
- 1 cup Vermont maple syrup
- 3 eggs
- 1 cup pecan halves (other nuts can be substituted), large pieces broken in two
- 1 nine-inch unbaked pie shell

Directions

1. Preheat oven to 375°.
2. Melt butter.
3. Add sugar, salt, syrup and eggs.
4. Beat until well blended.
5. Add pecans and pour filling into pie crust.
6. Bake 35 to 45 minutes.
7. Chill before serving.

Pie Pastry

Makes two pie crust shells

Ingredients

- 2 cups all-purpose sifted flour
- 1 teaspoon salt
- $\frac{3}{4}$ cup shortening
- 4 tablespoons cold water

To make one pie crust shell

Ingredients

- $1\frac{1}{4}$ cups of flour
- $\frac{1}{2}$ teaspoon salt
- $\frac{2}{3}$ cup shortening
- $2\frac{1}{2}$ tablespoons cold water

Directions

1. Mix flour and salt.
2. Cut in about 2/3 of the shortening with pastry blender until fine as meal.
3. Cut in rest of shortening until size of peas.
4. Sprinkle water over different parts of mixture.
5. Mix with a fork until it clings together.
6. Knead into 2 balls of dough.
7. Roll out on floured pastry cloth or surface.

Rhubarb Ring Cake with Maple Syrup Sauce

Serves 10

Ingredients

Cake

$\frac{1}{3}$ cup shortening

$1\frac{1}{2}$ cups white sugar

2 eggs

2 cups white flour

$1\frac{1}{2}$ teaspoons baking powder

$\frac{1}{8}$ teaspoon salt

$\frac{1}{4}$ cup milk

$\frac{1}{2}$ teaspoon vanilla

1 pound fresh raw rhubarb, cut into $\frac{1}{2}$-inch pieces

Sauce

1 cup maple syrup

1 teaspoon cornstarch

$\frac{3}{4}$ cup white sugar

$\frac{1}{8}$ teaspoon salt

$\frac{1}{4}$ teaspoon vanilla

4 tablespoons butter

Directions

1. Preheat oven to 375°.

2. In a bowl, beat shortening and sugar with an electric beater until light and fluffy.

3. Add eggs one at a time and continue beating until they are completely incorporated.

4. In a second bowl, sift together flour, baking powder, and salt.

5. In another bowl, mix the milk and vanilla together.

6. Alternately, add the flour mixture and the milk mixture to the shortening and eggs.

7. Fold in the raw rhubarb.

8. Pour mixture into a greased and floured tube pan.

9. Bake for 40 minutes.

10. In a saucepan, heat the maple syrup and add the cornstarch that has been mixed with a little water.

11. Add the sugar and salt; cook until slightly thickened.

12. Remove from the heat and add vanilla and butter.

13. Pour sauce over cooled caked.

Coconut Crème Brulée

Serves 8

Ingredients

$1\frac{3}{4}$ cups heavy cream

$1\frac{3}{4}$ cups milk

1 vanilla bean, split lengthwise

6 large egg yolks

$\frac{1}{2}$ cup granulated sugar

$\frac{2}{3}$ cup flaked coconut

$\frac{1}{4}$ cup light brown sugar

Directions

1. Preheat oven to 325°.

2. In saucepan, heat cream, milk, and vanilla bean until they come to a boil.

3. Whisk together egg yolks, sugar, and coconut.

4. Combine with cream.

5. Divide mixture into 8 ramekins and cook (water bath) in oven for about 40 minutes.

6. Let set for at least 4 hours.

7. Top with brown sugar and broil.

Almond Butter Cookies

Makes 2 dozen

Ingredients

Cookies

1 cup butter, softened

3 tablespoons sugar

1 teaspoon almond extract

2 cups sifted flour

$\frac{1}{4}$ teaspoon salt

Unblanched sliced almonds with skin on for garnish

Frosting

1 cup confectioners' sugar

1 tablespoon butter, softened

$\frac{1}{2}$ teaspoon vanilla

$1\frac{1}{2}$ tablespoons hot water

Directions

Cookies

1. Preheat oven to 350°.

2. Cream butter in large mixing bowl.

3. Add sugar and almond extract and beat well.

4. Sift together flour and salt.

5. Gradually add to creamed mixture.

6. For ease in handling, chill at least 30 minutes.

7. Shape into 1-inch balls and place on baking sheet.

8. Flatten to 1/4-inch thickness with bottom of glass dipped in flour.

9. Bake 10 to 12 minutes.

10. Cool, frost, decorate with sliced almonds.

Frosting

1. Stir all ingredients together in small bowl until smooth.

2. Frost each cookie with about 1/2 teaspoon frosting.

Fresh Strawberry Frosting

Ingredients

$\frac{1}{4}$ cup butter

2 cups confectioners' sugar

$\frac{1}{8}$ teaspoon salt

$\frac{1}{4}$ cup fresh strawberries, crushed

Directions

1. Cream butter and gradually add 1 cup sugar while stirring.

2. When butter and first cup of sugar are combined, add the second cup of sugar and salt, while alternating with the strawberries.

3. Add more sugar or crushed berries until proper consistency.

Frost your favorite cake!

Maple-Glazed Walnut Pound Cake

Serves 12

Ingredients

- 1¾ cups coarsely shopped walnuts
- 2¼ cups cake flour
- 1 teaspoon baking powder
- ½ teaspoon salt
- ¼ cup unsalted butter
- ¼ cup sugar
- 5 large eggs
- ½ cup pure maple syrup
- ½ teaspoon vanilla extract

Glaze

- ¼ cup unsalted butter
- 2 tablespoons pure maple syrup
- 2 tablespoons whipping cream
- 6 tablespoons powdered sugar
- 12 walnut halves

Directions

1. Preheat oven to 350°.
2. Finely grind walnuts in processor.
3. Sift flour, baking powder, and salt in medium bowl; set aside.
4. Beat butter and sugar until light and fluffy.
5. In a separate bowl, add eggs one at a time, beating in maple syrup and vanilla extract.
6. Mix in dry ingredients.
7. Fold in ground walnuts.
8. Pour into tube pan and bake for 35 minutes until a toothpick inserted in center comes out clean.

For Glaze

1. Melt butter with maple syrup and cream in heavy small saucepan. Remove from heat.
2. Add powdered sugar and whisk until smooth.
3. Cool glaze until slightly thickened, about 15 minutes.
4. Poke cake with a wire tester.
5. Drizzle glaze over pound cake.
6. Decorate with walnuts.

Summer

Frittata

Serves 6

Ingredients

- 2 tablespoons oil
- 2 cloves minced garlic
- 1 cup fresh mushrooms, sliced
- $\frac{2}{3}$ cup onion, chopped
- $\frac{2}{3}$ cup green pepper, chopped
- 1 cup chopped zucchini
- 5 eggs
- $\frac{1}{3}$ cup light cream
- $\frac{1}{2}$ teaspoon salt
- $\frac{1}{4}$ teaspoon pepper
- $1\frac{1}{2}$ cups soft bread cubes, lightly packed
- 8 ounces cream cheese cut in $\frac{1}{2}$-inch cubes
- 1 cup shredded cheddar cheese

Directions

1. Preheat oven to 350°.

2. Sauté the garlic in oil under medium heat; add mushrooms, onion, green pepper, and zucchini and sauté until tender; cool slightly.

3. In a separate bowl beat eggs, cream, salt, and pepper, add bread cubes and cheeses and mix.

4. Add sautéed vegetables to egg and bread mixture.

5. Pour into greased 9-inch pie plate.

6. Bake at 350° for about 45 minutes or until set.

This can be served for dinner or a luncheon; if you would like to serve it for an hors d'oeuvre, bake it in a square glass baking dish and cut into small squares.

Can be made ahead and frozen. If frozen, thaw completely before baking.

Warm Blueberry Crêpes with Vermont Maple Cream

Serves 10

Ingredients

Crêpes

- $\frac{3}{4}$ cup King Arthur unbleached all purpose flour
- $\frac{3}{4}$ cup King Arthur stoneground whole wheat flour
- 2 cups milk, 2% fat
- 3 tablespoons sugar
- 3 tablespoons corn oil
- 6 egg whites, slightly whipped
- 2 teaspoons baking powder

Blueberry filling

- 2 cups fresh blueberries
- $\frac{1}{2}$ cup orange juice
- 1 tablespoon cornstarch
- 1 tablespoon cold water

Maple Cream

- 1 cup Cabot lowfat cottage cheese
- 2 tablespoons maple syrup
- $\frac{1}{2}$ teaspoon orange rind
- $\frac{1}{8}$ teaspoon vanilla extract
- Pinch cinnamon
- Mint sprigs for garnish

Directions

Crêpes

1. Combine all ingredients in a bowl, mix until smooth, and let set for 10 minutes.

2. Place a nonstick pan over medium heat. Just before cooking, remove pan from heat and spray with 100% vegetable oil. Add 2 tablespoons of batter, turning the pan from side to side to coat the bottom with a thin layer.

3. Return pan to heat and cook until edges start to brown, approximately 2 to 3 minutes. Flip crêpe with a spatula and brown other side.

4. Make one crêpe for each person to be served.

Filling

1. Dissolve cornstarch in a small bowl with water. Set aside.

2. Place blueberries and orange juice in a saucepan over high heat and bring to boil. Add cornstarch mixture to berries, stirring constantly.

3. Mixture will immediately start to thicken. Lower heat and simmer 3 to 5 minutes. Remove and keep warm.

Maple Cream

1. Combine all ingredients in a blender and mix until smooth and creamy.

To serve lay one crêpe flat on a small plate, spoon 2 tablespoons of blueberry filling onto each, and roll into a tube shape. Top with 1 tablespoon of maple cream and garnish with a fresh blueberry and mint sprig.

Tofu Omelette with Mushrooms, Onions, and Cheese

Serves 4

Ingredients

- 1 cup Tofu (firm)
- 3 egg whites
- $\frac{1}{8}$ teaspoon garlic powder
- $\frac{1}{8}$ teaspoon paprika
- 2 tablespoons low-sodium Lite Soy Sauce
- $\frac{1}{2}$ cup mushrooms, sliced
- $\frac{1}{4}$ cup onion, diced
- $\frac{1}{3}$ cup Cabot Vitalait Cheese, (or other low fat cheddar cheese) grated

Directions

1. Remove tofu from water and squeeze dry in a strainer. If possible let the tofu drain in the refrigerator overnight.

2. Add egg whites, garlic, paprika, and soy sauce to tofu and mix in a blender or Cuisinart until smooth.

3. Sauté the mushrooms and onions until tender.

4. Take 1/4 of the tofu mixture and add it to a pan with 1/4 of the mushroom and onion mixture, spread in a circle, and cook over medium heat until golden brown. Then flip and brown other side.

5. Place omelette on an oven-proof dish and top with 1 tablespoon of cheese and put under broiler until cheese is melted. Serve at once.

Clam Crisps

Makes 12 1/2 Dozen

Ingredients

- 1 cup flour
- 1 teaspoon baking powder
- $\frac{1}{4}$ teaspoon cayenne pepper
- 2 eggs
- $\frac{1}{2}$ cup milk
- 2 cups chopped clams, freshly shucked or canned
- $\frac{1}{4}$ cup finely chopped shallots
- 1 teaspoon finely chopped parsley
- Salt and pepper to taste
- Vegetable oil for deep frying

Directions

1. Sift the dry ingredients together in a bowl.

2. In another bowl, mix remaining ingredients until just blended.

3. Add the flour mixture to form dough. Let dough rest for 30 minutes.

4. Drop tablespoon of dough into 375° hot oil of a deep fryer.

5. Cook until golden. Drain on paper towel. Serve immediately.

Roasted Red Pepper Dip

Makes 1 1/2 cups

Ingredients

12 ounces red bell peppers, roasted, peeled, and seeds removed

1 whole head roasted garlic, pulp squeezed and skins discarded

8 ounces soft goat cheese

3 tablespoons olive oil

4 tablespoons minced fresh basil

2 teaspoons chopped fresh rosemary

$\frac{1}{8}$ teaspoon cayenne

$\frac{1}{2}$ teaspoon salt

$\frac{1}{4}$ teaspoon pepper

Vegetables for dipping

Directions

1. Puree red peppers, garlic, and cheese in food processor or blender until smooth.

2. Stir in remaining ingredients.

3. Cover and refrigerate to make firm.

4. Serve with vegetables for dipping.

Prince Edward Island Mussels with Thai-Style Coconut Curry

Serves 4

Ingredients

- 4 pounds Prince Edward Island mussels
- 1 medium onion
- 1 teaspoon peanut oil
- 1 tablespoon red Thai curry paste or to taste
- 1 can coconut milk (14 ounces)
- 1 tablespoon thinly sliced lemon grass
- 2 kaffar lime leaves (optional)
- 2 tablespoons freshly chopped cilantro
- 2 tablespoons thinly sliced scallions
- 2 tablespoons Thai lemon basil (optional)

  Juice of 1 lime

Directions

1. Chop and sauté the onion in the peanut oil.

2. Stir in the curry paste, add the can of coconut milk and an equal amount of water. Add the lemon grass.

3. Simmer for 10 minutes or so.

4. The mixture can be cooled and blended if desired at this time. Pour mixture back into the pot and add the cleaned and debearded mussels to the liquid. Cover and steam the mussels until they open (do not overcook).

5. Spoon out the mussels into four large bowls, leaving the liquid in the pot.

6. Add the lime leaves, lime juice, cilantro, scallions, and lemon basil to the curry sauce and divide evenly over the mussels. Serve immediately.

Clams Casino

Serves 6 to 8 as an appetizer

Ingredients

$\frac{1}{2}$ pound unsalted butter

2 cloves garlic

1 tablespoon dry white wine

1 tablespoon fresh lemon juice

1 tablespoon shallots, finely chopped

1 teaspoon parsley, finely chopped

Pinch fresh ground pepper

$\frac{1}{4}$ pound Pancetta (very thinly sliced)

$\frac{1}{8}$ pound Asiago (graded)

24 Little Neck Clams (medium-large)

Directions

1. Whip butter at room temperature with whisk or electric mixer.

2. When butter is a smooth consistency, add garlic (pressed or finely chopped), white wine, lemon juice, shallots, parsley and pepper. Mix well for 2 minutes. Place to side ensuring it stays at the same consistency.

3. Clean and shuck clams and place on a heavy baking sheet.

4. Add a dollop (about 1/2 teaspoon more or less) of butter to each clam. Add small strips of Pancetta to cover clam, then add a few pinches of Asiago to cover Pancetta.

5. Either bake at high temperature (450°) or broil until cheese melts—no more than 4 to 5 minutes in oven or two minutes under broiler. (Do not overcook or clams will be like rubber.)

6. Serve with lemon and place white napkin on serving dish to prevent clams from sliding.

Smoked Salmon Mousse

Serves 12

Ingredients

8 ounces smoked salmon

½ cup plain yogurt

⅛ teaspoon cayenne pepper

½ teaspoon paprika

2 tablespoons extra-virgin olive oil

1 lemon

Directions

1. Roughly chop half the salmon and put in food processor.

2. Add yogurt, cayenne, paprika, and olive oil.

3. Juice and grate zest of lemon.

4. Add lemon zest and 2 tablespoons of lemon juice and process to form purée.

5. Transfer to bowl.

6. Coarsely chop remaining salmon and add to purée.

7. Mix well, cover, and refrigerate until serving time.

Sweet Corn Chowder

Serves 8

Ingredients

$\frac{1}{4}$ pound salt pork cut in $\frac{1}{4}$-inch cubes (optional) or 4 tablespoons olive oil

2 large Spanish onions, chopped

2 quarts whole milk

2 pounds Yukon Gold potatoes, peeled and diced

$\frac{1}{2}$ teaspoon Kosher salt

6 ears very fresh Silver Queen corn

3 tablespoons broadleaf parsley, chopped

1 red pepper, chopped and sautéed

$\frac{1}{2}$ teaspoon fresh cracked black pepper

Directions

1. Sauté salt pork until crisp, then set aside.

2. Pour off all but 2 tablespoons fat (or olive oil).

3. Add chopped onion and sauté until translucent.

4. Add milk, potatoes, and salt.

5. Simmer until potatoes are just soft, stirring occasionally (do not let milk boil).

7. Puree 4 cups of this mixture in blender, including potatoes, until smooth.

8. Return to pot after each batch.

9. Add corn cut from cob, parsley, red pepper, cracked pepper; salt to taste and simmer slightly.

10. Garnish with crispy pork and more parsley, if desired.

Chilled Pea Soup

Serves 6 to 8

Ingredients

- 1 cup onion
- 1 cup celery
- 2 tablespoons butter
- 5 cups hulled fresh peas, approximately 5 pounds
- 5 cups chicken stock
- $1\frac{1}{2}$ cups heavy cream
- $\frac{1}{2}$ teaspoon salt
- $\frac{1}{4}$ teaspoon pepper
- Mint for garnish

Directions

1. Place the onion and celery in a 4-quart pot with 2 tablespoons of butter. Cook 5 minutes over low heat stirring occasionally.

2. Add the peas and stock to the onion mixture. Bring to simmer.

3. Once the peas are soft, puree soup in a blender and pass it through a food mill using the fine grate.

4. Pour soup into a large bowl and chill.

5. Stir in the cream; mix well.

6. Add salt and pepper. Serve in chilled cups and garnish with mint.

Gazpacho

Serves 4 to 6 (two blenders full)

Ingredients

- 6 large tomatoes
- 1 garlic clove
- $\frac{1}{2}$ cucumber
- $\frac{1}{4}$ teaspoon salt
- 1 cup olive oil
- 2 tablespoons sherry vinegar
- $\frac{1}{2}$ green pepper
- 1 slice French bread (for texture)
- Croutons

Directions

1. Chop vegetables.
2. Place 1/2 of all ingredients in blender.
3. Blend until smooth.
4. Place remaining ingredients in blend.
5. Blend until smooth.
6. Serve in bowls and garnish with diced green peppers, cucumbers, and croutons.

Cold Cream of Zucchini Soup

Serves 6

Ingredients

$2\frac{1}{2}$ pounds small zucchini,
1 julienned, the rest chopped

1 cup chopped onions

1 clove garlic, minced

1 teaspoon good-quality curry powder

3 cups chicken or vegetable stock

2 cups half-and-half

Salt and pepper to taste

2 tablespoons chopped chives

Directions

1. Place julienned zucchini in strainer and set aside.

2. Place remaining zucchini in soup pot with onions, garlic, curry powder, and stock.

3. Bring to boil, lower heat, and simmer 45 minutes.

4. While soup is boiling, lower strainer with julienned zucchini into it for 1 minute.

5. Blend in food processor with half-and-half.

6. Adjust seasonings and chill.

7. Serve with julienned zucchini and chives sprinkled on top.

Chilled Almond Soup

Serves 4

Ingredients

1 large leek (white part only) thinly sliced

$\frac{1}{2}$ cup celery, diced

1 tablespoon butter

1 quart strong, hot chicken stock

1 tablespoon rice, rinsed and drained

1 cup finely ground blanched almonds

$1\frac{1}{4}$ cups heavy cream

Salt and pepper

Toasted sliced almonds

Directions

1. Place the leeks and celery in a 2- quart pot with the butter and 1 tablespoon of the stock. Cook 5 minutes over low heat, covered. Stir occasionally.

2. Pour the hot chicken stock over it and bring to a boil.

3. Add the rice and ground almonds. Cover the pot, reduce heat to low, and cook 30 minutes, keeping the broth just under a simmer.

4. After the soup has cooked 30 minutes, puree it in a blender and pass it through a food mill using the find grate.

5. Pour the soup into a clean 2-quart bowl and chill.

6. Stir in the cream; mix well.

7. Add salt and pepper to taste.

8. Serve in chilled cups and garnish with sliced almonds.

Indian Cucumber Salad

Serves 6

Ingredients

3 sliced cucumbers

1 small red onion, diced

3 tablespoons canola oil

2 teaspoons minced garlic

$\frac{1}{2}$ teaspoon ground cumin

$\frac{1}{2}$ teaspoon ground ginger

Pinch of fenugreek

$\frac{1}{4}$ teaspoon ground coriander seed

Pinch ground cardamon

$\frac{2}{3}$ cup nonfat plain yogurt

$\frac{1}{2}$ teaspoon chili-garlic paste

Directions

Hint: Collect and measure all spices before heating the oil, making two mixtures; ginger/cumin mixture and the fenugreek, coriander, and cardamon mixture.

1. Heat canola oil in a sauté pan.

2. Sauté red onion until just soft, but still colored.

3. Add ginger and cumin and cook over medium heat for 1 minute.

4. Add minced garlic and remaining spice mixture and sauté briefly until garlic becomes fragrant.

5. Remove from heat and add chili-garlic paste and yogurt; whisk until very smooth.

6. Pour over sliced cucumbers and toss until the cucumbers are evenly coated. Chill at least 15 minutes before serving.

Bruschetta with Tomatoes and Basil

Serves 8

Ingredients

- 2 pounds ripe tomatoes, cut into $\frac{1}{4}$-inch dice
- 2 tablespoons minced shallots
- 1 cup fresh basil leaves, coarsely chopped
- 1 teaspoon balsamic vinegar
- $\frac{1}{2}$ teaspoon salt
- $\frac{1}{4}$ teaspoon freshly ground pepper
- $\frac{2}{3}$ cup olive oil (set aside $\frac{1}{3}$ cup)
- 3 cloves garlic, cut in half
- 1 loaf of sourdough, farm bread, or baguette

Directions

1. Toss together the tomatoes, shallots, basil, balsamic vinegar, salt, pepper, and 1/3 cup of olive oil in large bowl. Set aside.

2. Heat remaining 1/3 cup of olive oil in a small skillet. Crush the garlic and sauté lightly for 2 to 3 minutes. Discard the garlic.

3. Grill or lightly toast the bread slices. Brush the garlic-flavored oil over each slice and top it with a healthy spoonful of the tomato mixture. Serve immediately.

You can top with parmesan cheese or shredded mozzarella, melted.

Soy Sesame Vinaigrette

Serves 6

Ingredients

$\frac{1}{4}$ cup olive oil

$2\frac{1}{2}$ tablespoons tarragon vinegar

$2\frac{1}{2}$ tablespoons soy sauce

$\frac{1}{4}$ teaspoon tightly packed tarragon leaves

$\frac{1}{8}$ teaspoon coarse salt

$\frac{1}{8}$ teaspoon dry mustard

$\frac{1}{8}$ teaspoon sesame oil

Freshly ground pepper to taste

Directions

Mix all ingredients and serve on bib lettuce.

Tomato Salad

Serves 4

Ingredients

6 ripe tomatoes (looks nice to mix red and golden)

3 tablespoons red wine vinegar

$\frac{1}{2}$ cup olive oil

2 teaspoons salt

1 teaspoon pepper

Dash dry mustard

2 tablespoons chopped fresh chives

2 tablespoons chopped fresh broadleaf parsley

1 tablespoon chopped fresh basil

Directions

1. Slice tomatoes and arrange on a serving platter.

2. Whisk together remaining ingredients and pour over tomatoes.

3. Serve at room temperature.

Warm Eggplant Salad

Serves 6

Ingredients

- 4 small unpeeled eggplants, cut into 1-inch cubes
- Salt
- Flour for dusting
- 2 cups olive oil
- $\frac{1}{2}$ cup extra-virgin olive oil
- 6 anchovies, chopped
- 4 sundried tomatoes, chopped
- 4 tablespoons balsamic vinegar
- 4 cloves garlic, chopped
- 1 tablespoon capers, drained
- $\frac{1}{4}$ cup chopped parsley
- Freshly ground black pepper

Directions

1. Sprinkle eggplant generously with salt and let drain in a colander for 30 minutes. Rinse and dry thoroughly.

2. In a bowl, mix the eggplant with some flour until lightly coated.

3. In a deep fryer, heat 2 cups of olive oil to 375°.

4. Deep-fry the eggplant in batches until golden, approximately 5 minutes.

5. Drain on paper towels.

6. In a saucepan, heat the olive oil over medium heat, stir in the anchovies, tomatoes, capers, vinegar and garlic and cook for 2 minutes.

7. Remove from heat and stir in the parsley and pepper to taste.

8. Transfer the eggplant to a serving plate and top with the dressing.

Zucchini Latkes

Serves 4

Ingredients

2 cups, zucchini, julienne cut or coarsely grated

$\frac{1}{2}$ cup flour, sifted with $\frac{1}{2}$ teaspoon baking powder

$\frac{1}{4}$ cup chopped onion

1 clove of garlic, minced

2 eggs

$\frac{1}{4}$ teaspoon salt

$\frac{1}{8}$ teaspoon pepper

$\frac{1}{8}$ teaspoon nutmeg

Oil for frying

Directions

1. Season the grated zucchini with salt, pepper, and nutmeg to taste. Let stand for 5 minutes. Squeeze out the excess liquid.

2. In a bowl, mix the eggs and add the zucchini, onions, and garlic.

3. Fold in the flour.

4. Heat oil in a frying pan. When hot, spoon the mixture into oil, making small round patties. Fry until golden brown, then turn over and brown the other side.

Corn Pudding

Serves 4

Ingredients

3 large eggs

¾ cup sugar

2 scant tablespoons flour

1 teaspoon vanilla

Dash of salt

16 ounces of half-and-half

1 15-ounce can whole kernel corn

Cinnamon

Directions

1. Preheat oven to 325°.

2. Drain corn and spread evenly on bottom of a baking dish.

3. Beat 3 eggs.

4. Mix flour into the sugar and add to the beaten eggs; mix until blended.

5. Add salt and vanilla to the mixture and stir.

6. Add half-and-half; stir together and pour over the corn.

7. Sprinkle with cinnamon.

8. Bake for 45 to 50 minutes or until mixture becomes "custard-like."

Peach and Ginger Chutney

Ingredients

- 7 large peaches, peeled and diced

- 1 large onion, finely chopped

- 1 yellow pepper, seeded and diced

- 1 hot red pepper, seeded and diced

- $\frac{1}{2}$ cup crystallized ginger, chopped

- 2 cups cider vinegar

- 3 cups sugar

- 1 teaspoon cinnamon

- $\frac{1}{4}$ teaspoon ground cloves

- $\frac{1}{4}$ teaspoon mace

Directions

1. In a saucepan, mix all the ingredients and bring to a boil.

2. Lower heat and simmer for 15 minutes or until all the vegetables are tender and the chutney has thickened.

Serve with roast pork, barbequed ribs, or grilled shrimp.

Greek Potato Salad

Serves 6 to 8

Ingredients

3 pounds small new potatoes

1 green pepper, seeded and coarsely chopped

1 bunch scallions, thinly sliced

2 small garden cucumbers, peeled and chopped

10-20 Kalamata olives, preferably pitted

$\frac{3}{4}$-1 pound feta cheese (to taste)

freshly ground pepper

Salt

$\frac{1}{2}$ cup olive oil

Juice of 1 lemon

Directions

1. Scrub potatoes and place in pot of salted cold water to cover.

2. Bring to boil, reduce heat to moderate, cover and cook 10 minutes or until just tender.

3. Drain, cut in half, place in bowl to cool slightly.

4. Add green pepper, scallions, cucumbers, olives, feta cheese, salt, and pepper.

5. Blend olive oil and lemon juice and pour over salad.

6. Toss gently and serve at room temperature.

Linguine with Lemon Sauce

Serves 6

Ingredients

- 1 pound linguini pasta
- 2 teaspoons fresh lemon rind, grated
- 1¼ sticks unsalted butter
- 2 tablespoons white wine
- 1⅔ cups heavy cream
- ⅛ teaspoon cayenne pepper
- 2 teaspoons fresh lemon juice
- ⅓ cup Parmesan cheese, grated

Directions

1. Cook the pasta in plenty of salted boiling water until *al dente,* then drain.

2. While pasta is cooking, heat a fry pan over medium heat, add 5 tablespoons of butter and heat for 1 minute.

3. Add the wine and cook for 30 seconds.

4. Add the cream and cayenne, cook for 2 minutes, stirring constantly.

5. Add pasta to the mixture.

6. Cook for 1 more minute.

7. Remove from heat and add remaining butter that has been cut into pieces.

8. Stir in lemon juice, parmesan, and salt and pepper to taste.

Excellent side dish with grilled shrimp.

Cheese Tortellini Salad with Pesto Dressing

Serves 6

Ingredients

- 1 pound cheese tortellini
- $\frac{1}{4}$ cup pesto
- 6 tablespoons olive oil
- 1 tablespoon fresh lemon juice
- 2 tablespoons balsamic vinegar
- 1 pound fresh clean spinach, stems removed
- 1 cup red onion, very thinly sliced
- $\frac{1}{4}$ cup pine nuts
- $\frac{1}{2}$ cup Gorgonzola cheese, crumbled

  Salt and pepper to taste

Directions

1. Cook tortellini in plenty of salted boiling water according to package directions.

2. In a large salad bowl, mix the pesto with 3 tablespoons olive oil and lemon juice.

3. Add tortellini and mix gently.

4. In a second bowl, combine remaining 3 tablespoons of olive oil, vinegar, salt, and pepper. Beat with a fork.

5. Add spinach to the dressing and toss.

6. On a large platter, make a bed of spinach and place the tortellini on top.

7. Garnish with pine nuts and sprinkle with Gorgonzola.

Mediterranean Potato Salad

Serves 10 to 12

Ingredients

- 4 pounds small red bliss potatoes, scrubbed but not peeled
- 6-8 large eggs, hard-cooked, shelled and coarsely chopped
- $\frac{3}{4}$ cup minced red onion
- $\frac{3}{4}$ cup chopped scallions
- $\frac{1}{2}$ cup capers, drained
- 4 pounds tomatoes, chopped

Dressing

- 1 cup best-quality olive oil
- $\frac{1}{4}$ cup balsamic vinegar
- 1 garlic clove, crushed
- 1 teaspoon salt
- $\frac{1}{2}$ teaspoon pepper
- $1\frac{1}{2}$ teaspoons fennel seeds
- $\frac{1}{8}$ teaspoon sage

Directions

1. Place potatoes in large pot and add cold water to cover.
2. Simmer uncovered until fork tender, about 25 minutes.
3. Drain and let cool.
4. Cut potatoes into large bite-size chunks.
5. Toss with eggs, onions, scallions, capers and tomatoes.

Dressing

1. Whisk together vinegar, garlic, fennel and sage in a medium bowl.
2. Whisk in oil.
3. Add salt and pepper.
4. Pour over potatoes and toss to combine.
5. Refrigerate until ready to serve.

Baked Zucchini

Serves 8 to 10

Ingredients

4-5 zucchini, average size (1$\frac{1}{2}$" x 8")

1 cup Parmesan cheese, grated

1 cup heavy cream

2 teaspoons Crazy Jane's Mixed-up Salt

Directions

1. Preheat oven to 375°.

2. Slice the zucchini thinly (1/8-inch slices) and stack it on edge in a 10x13-inch baking dish.

3. Fan the zucchini slices out slightly so that they are not stacked vertically. This will enable you to expose a greater portion of each slice for the Parmesan cheese to grab onto.

4. Pour 2/3 cup of heavy cream evenly over the zucchini.

5. Sprinkle Parmesan cheese evenly over zucchini.

6. Delicately pour the remainder of the heavy cream over the zucchini and Parmesan mixture. You do not want to wash off the Parmesan already on the zucchini.

7. Sprinkle the crazy salt over the zucchini and bake at 375° for 25 minutes.

8. The zucchini should be browned around the edges and cooked through.

9. Once cooked, the zucchini may be moved to a serving dish, but it's best served directly from the baking dish.

Marinated Pork Tenderloin

Serves 6

Ingredients

4 12-ounce pork tenderloins

$\frac{1}{2}$ cup soy sauce

$\frac{3}{4}$ cup lemon juice

6 tablespoons honey

1 small onion, finely chopped

1 teaspoon minced garlic

2 bay leaves, crumbled

2 teaspoons salt

2 teaspoons pepper

1 teaspoon Dijon mustard

$\frac{1}{2}$ teaspoon ground ginger

Directions

1. Combine all the marinated ingredients.

2. Marinate pork in mixture in a sealed or covered container in the refrigerator overnight.

3. Remove pork from liquid and pour marinade into a saucepan.

4. Grill pork over medium-high heat, turning frequently, for about 20 minutes.

5. While grilling the pork, boil the marinade until reduced to a sauce consistency, about 5 minutes.

6. Slice pork and serve with sauce.

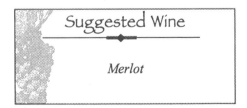

Suggested Wine

Merlot

Grilled Tuna Verde Topped with an Avocado Aioli

Serves 4

Ingredients

4 8-ounce tuna steaks

Marinade for Tuna

1 cup thinly sliced green onions or scallions

¾ cup packed fresh cilantro leaves

3 tablespoons olive oil

3 tablespoons fresh lime juice

1½ tablespoons grated lime peel

1½ tablespoons brown sugar

1 tablespoon coarsely chopped jalapeño peppers, seeds included

Avocado Aioli

1 large ripe avocado, pitted and flesh removed from skin

2 cloves of garlic, minced

4 tablespoons mayonnaise

1 tablespoon fresh lime juice

Several dashes of Tabasco

Directions

Marinade

1. In food processor blend ingredients until almost smooth. Season with salt and pepper.

2. Pour marinade into a shallow glass baking dish and add tuna, turning to coat.

3. Cover; let stand at room temperature 1 hour or refrigerate for 2 hours, turning tuna several times to let marinade soak in.

Avocado Aioli

1. Purée all ingredients in a food processor, scraping down sides occasionally; season with salt and pepper.

2. Cover and chill until tuna is ready to be served. Can be made up to 4 hours ahead.

Tuna

1. Grill fish over medium-heat barbecue for 4 minutes on each side, or to one's liking, basting often with marinade.

2. Garnish with Avocado Aioli and serve at once.

Boneless chicken breast or any other seafood steak can be used instead of tuna.

Suggested Wine

*Slightly off-dry Riesling
Gewürztraminer*

Pasta with Arugula

Serves 4

Ingredients

1 pound fussili

4 cups heavy cream

1 large bunch basil, coarsely chopped

$1\frac{1}{2}$ teaspoons fresh black ground pepper

3-4 large cloves garlic, finely chopped

3 cups grated Parmesan or Romano cheese (or mixture)

4-5 bunches arugula, well cleaned and stems removed

2 pints cherry tomatoes, halved or 4 medium tomatoes, peeled and diced

$\frac{1}{4}$ teaspoon salt

$\frac{1}{8}$ teaspoon pepper

Directions

1. Cook fussili according to directions.

2. Simmer cream, basil, pepper, and garlic.

3. Add drained pasta to sauce.

4. Add cheese(s), arugula, and tomatoes.

5. Serve immediately.

Suggested Wine

*Rich Sauvignon Blanc
Sangiovese*

Soft Shell Crabs with Thai Ginger and Buckwheat Noodles

Serves 4

Ingredients

8 soft shell crabs with the gills and eyes removed

2 tablespoons galunga (Thai ginger) peeled and chopped (fresh ginger may be substituted)

2 large shallots

3 tablespoons lime juice

2 tablespoons raw sugar

4 tablespoons fish sauce

1 green jalapeño

8 ounces buckwheat noodles

Peanut oil for sauté

Cornstarch for coating

2 tablespoons fresh cilantro

Directions

1. Have your fishmonger clean the crabs. Pat dry and set aside.

2. To make "ginger sauce", add the next 6 ingredients to blender or food processor and blend until finely chopped but not smooth. Set aside.

Suggested Wine

Sauvignon Blanc
Gewürztraminer

3. Cook the noodles and rinse to cool. Drain and dry well.

4. Heat an 8-inch non-stick sauté pan and add oil to just cover the bottom. Just before oil smokes, gently lay some noodles to cover the surface of the pan (there should be some holes in the "pancake". Gently fry the noodles until golden. Flip the cake and fry the other side until golden.

5. Remove from the pan and drain on a towel.

6. Repeat again 3 times, so you have 4 noodle cakes. Keep warm.

7. Dredge the crabs in cornstarch.

8. Heat a large sauté pan. Add oil to cover the bottom and continue heating until oil almost smokes.

9. Gently lay the crabs back-side down in the pan. Cover loosely to prevent spatter and cook until crispy and golden. Turn and repeat for the belly.

10. When done, set the noodle cake on a dinner plate then 2 crabs on top of the noodle cake. Set the 4 plates in warm place.

11. Turn down the heat and add the *ginger sauce* to the pan with the oil. Bring to a boil and pour over each crab.

12. Garnish with cilantro and serve at once.

Corn and Shrimp Salad

Serves 4

Ingredients

28-36 medium to large shrimp,
  peeled and deveined

  Shrimp Boil or Old Bay Seasoning

1 can of black beans, drained

1½ cups corn kernels, barely cooked

Marinade:

¾ cup olive oil

½ cup red wine vinegar

1½ tablespoons Dijon mustard

1½ tablespoons chives

1½ tablespoons parsley

½ tablespoon minced shallot

Directions

1. Bring 3 inches of water to boil in a saucepan with "Shrimp Boil."

2. Add shrimp, cook 1 to 2 minutes.

3. Cool in liquid in saucepan, then drain.

4. Marinate in refrigerator 2 hours or more.

5. Before serving add beans and corn.

6. Serve on mixed greens; drain if necessary.

If doubled, reduce liquid accordingly.

Summer Risotto with Chanterelles and Peas

Serves 4

Ingredients

- ¾ pound chanterelles
- 1 medium onion
- 2 shallots
- 1½ cups arborio rice
- 1½ teaspoons salt
- ¼ teaspoon black pepper
- 6 cups vegetable stock (chicken will work)
- 1 cup white wine
- 8 baby carrots (if available)
- 2 tablespoons chervil or tarragon
- 1 cup shelled peas
- 1 cup grated firm sheep's milk cheese or Parmesan
- Olive oil for sauté

Directions

1. Clean the chanterelles with a soft brush, using water only if the mushrooms are very gritty.

2. Chop the onions and shallots and sauté in olive oil in a 2-quart saucepan until soft but not browned.

3. Add the chanterelles and toss well.

4. Add the rice and stir until rice is translucent.

5. Add salt, pepper, 2 cups stock, and wine, stirring constantly, adding more stock as liquid is absorbed. Rice is done when it is creamy but still slightly "al dente" in the center.

6. Start to cook carrots in cold water and bring to a boil. Boil until done, remove. Add peas to boiling water and cook until tender.

7. Stir the peas, chervil, and cheese into rice.

8. Arrange the carrots around the top and serve with cheese.

Suggested Wine

Pinot Noir
Sangiovese
Riosa

Chicken Salad

Serves 6

Ingredients

$1\frac{1}{2}$ cups pasta shells, cooked

2 cups cooked, cubed chicken

1 cup chopped celery

$\frac{1}{2}$ teaspoon salt

$\frac{1}{4}$ teaspoon pepper

$\frac{1}{3}$ cup white wine

$1\frac{1}{2}$ tablespoons lemon juice
(juice of $\frac{1}{2}$ lemon)

1 cup seedless grapes

$\frac{1}{4}$ pound toasted, sliced almonds

$\frac{3}{4}$ to 1 cup mayonnaise

Directions

1. Combine pasta shells and chicken.

2. Combine wine, lemon juice, salt, and pepper in a separate bowl.

3. Pour over chicken mixture and marinate at least 4 hours.

4. Add mayonnaise and remaining ingredients.

Suggested Wine

Rich Chardonnay

Glazed Fish Steaks

Serves 4

Ingredients

- 4 6-ounce tuna or salmon steaks
- 2 tablespoons fresh lime juice
- 1½ tablespoons soy sauce
- 2 garlic cloves, crushed
- 2 teaspoons ginger root, peeled and grated
- 1½ teaspoons sesame oil
- 1 teaspoon Jalapeño pepper, minced and seeded
- ½ teaspoon sugar

Directions

1. Place fish in baking dish.
2. Whisk remaining ingredients together and pour over fish, turning to coat.
3. Cover with plastic wrap and marinate in refrigerator 1 hour, turning occasionally.
4. Preheat broiler or grill.
5. Transfer fish to broiler pan or grill.
6. Grill, basting and turning often, until done—approximately 10 minutes.

Suggested Wine

Riesling
Pinot Noir

Lemon Veal

Serves 4

Ingredients

16 slices of veal scaloppine
   (1 ounce each)

2 ounces white wine

Juice of 2 lemons

2 ounces olive oil

2 tablespoons capers

2 ounces unsalted butter

2 ounces chopped parsley

Directions

1. Inside a separate pan, warm
   2 ounces olive oil.

2. Dredge scaloppine into white
   all-purpose flour, shake off excess,
   then sauté for 30 seconds on each
   side. When all cooked, remove
   from pan. Let rest.

3. In another pan, melt butter, add
   capers, lemon juice and a touch of
   white wine, reduce.

4. Then add veal and let rest inside
   for 5 minutes before serving.

Suggested Wine

Pinot Gris (Grigio)
Sauvignon Blanc

Tandoori Chicken

Serves 8 to 10

Ingredients

- 5 pounds chicken breasts, boneless and skinless
- 3 teaspoons fresh garlic, finely chopped
- 2 teaspoons fresh ginger, finely chopped
- 2 pounds plain yogurt or a bit less
- $\frac{1}{8}$ teaspoon ground red pepper
- 1 tablespoon salt
- 8 ounces (2/3 jar) Tandoori paste

Directions

1. Mix together all except chicken.
2. Add chicken and marinate 2 to 3 hours in refrigerator.
3. Remove chicken from marinade and grill, discarding remaining marinade.

Suggested Wine

Off-dry Chenin Blanc or Riesling
Red Zinfandel

Roasted Vegetable Orzo Salad

Serves 6

Ingredients

- 1 1-pound package of orzo
- $\frac{1}{2}$ cup pignoli nuts
- $\frac{1}{2}$-1 cup feta cheese
- 2 tablespoons chopped parsley
- 1 cup red onion, cut lengthwise into 1-inch pieces
- 2 cups red peppers, cut into 1-inch pieces
- 1 cup yellow pepper, cut into 1-inch pieces
- 2 cups cubed eggplant
- 2 cups sliced zucchini
- 1 tablespoon chopped shallots
- 1-2 tablespoons infused olive oil (basil, rosemary, garlic, etc.)

Directions

1. Cook orzo according to package directions.
2. Roast vegetables (grill or oven method).
3. Sauté pignoli nuts until brown.
4. Mix roasted vegetables with orzo.
5. Add pignoli nuts, feta cheese, parsley to taste.
6. Moisten with infused olive oil, or favorite oil dressing.

Suggested Wine

Sauvignon Blanc
Côtes du Rhône
Rioja

Grilled Swordfish and Tomato Herb Salsa

Serves 4

Ingredients

1 pound Swordfish

Marinade

$\frac{1}{2}$ cup fresh lime juice

$\frac{1}{2}$ teaspoon ground white pepper

$1\frac{1}{4}$ cups of water

$\frac{1}{2}$ teaspoon cumin

$\frac{3}{4}$ teaspoon oregano

1 clove of garlic, minced

$\frac{1}{2}$ teaspoon salt

$\frac{1}{2}$ teaspoon sugar

2 bay leaves

1 red chili pepper, chopped or $\frac{1}{8}$ teaspoon chili pepper flakes

1 tablespoon extra-virgin olive oil

1 medium onion, finely diced

Tomato Herb Salsa

4 medium tomatoes, very ripe

1 teaspoon cracked coriander seed

3 teaspoons extra-virgin olive oil

1 tablespoon fresh cilantro, chopped

Juice of 1 lemon

1 tablespoon fresh chives, sliced

2 tablespoons onion, minced

$\frac{1}{4}$ teaspoon ground white pepper

$\frac{1}{8}$ teaspoon salt (optional)

4 drops Tabasco

Directions

1. Cut swordfish into 4-ounce portions and marinate for 1 to 2 hours in refrigerator.

2. While fish is marinating, prepare salsa.

3. First core tomatoes then drop into boiling water for 10 seconds. Remove and drop into cold water. Remove from water and peel skin using a small paring knife. Remove seeds and chop finely.

4. Place tomatoes and remaining ingredients in a bowl and mix well. Keep at room temperature.

5. Grill fish for a total of 5 to 10 minutes depending upon thickness, turning once. Swordfish should be slightly pink inside. Be careful not to overcook since swordfish can become dry.

6. Serve each piece of fish with 4 tablespoons of salsa and garnish with fresh cilantro and lemon slices.

Suggested Wine

Sauvignon Blanc
Pinot Noir

Barbecue Spareribs

Serves 4

Ingredients

3-4 pounds ribs, cut in pieces

1 lemon

1 large onion

1 cup catsup

$\frac{1}{3}$ cup Worcestershire Sauce

1 teaspoon chili powder

1 teaspoon salt

2 dashes Tabasco Sauce

2 cups water

Directions

1. Preheat oven to 450°.

2. Place ribs in shallow roasting pan, meaty side up.

3. On each piece of rib, place a slice of unpeeled lemon and a thin slice of onion.

4. Roast in hot oven for 30 minutes.

5. Combine remaining ingredients, heat to boiling, and pour over ribs.

6. Reduce oven temperature to 350° and continue baking until tender, about 45 minutes to one hour.

Baste ribs with sauce every 15 minutes.

Suggested Wine

Red Zinfandel
Syrah

Marinated Butterflied Baby Leg of Lamb

Serves 6 to 8

Ingredients for Marinade

Approximately 3 pounds boneless butterflied leg of lamb

$\frac{2}{3}$ cup soy sauce

$\frac{1}{4}$ cup olive oil

6 cloves garlic, minced

2 teaspoons ginger

2 teaspoons dry mustard or Dijon

2 tablespoons molasses

Directions

1. Mix all ingredients.

2. Fork-prick lamb thoroughly on both sides.

3. Marinate lamb for 24 hours, turning occasionally, spooning sauce over meat.

Preheat grill. Grill meat about 10 minutes on both sides.

Suggested Wine

Cabernet Sauvignon
Red Bordeaux

Chocolate Mousse Cake

Serves 10 to 12

Ingredients

- 1 pound chocolate chips
- 1 pound butter
- 1 cup sugar
- 1 cup half-and-half
- 8 eggs
- 1 tablespoon vanilla
- 1 teaspoon salt

Topping - Ingredients

- 1 cup cream
- 1 tablespoon sugar
- 8 ounces chocolate chips

Directions

1. Preheat oven to 350°.
2. Melt chocolate, sugar, butter, and half-and-half in a double boiler.
3. Don't allow it to get too hot (80° maximum).
4. Whip eggs, vanilla, and salt.
5. Add chocolate mixture while whipping slowly.
6. Bake at 350° for 45 minutes in a water bath in 10-inch cake pan lined with parchment paper.
7. Once cake has cooled, frost with chocolate topping.

Topping Directions

1. Heat cream and sugar; pour over chocolate chips.
2. Blend thoroughly.

Trifle

Serves: 8

Ingredients

Sponge Cake

$\frac{3}{4}$ cup sifted cake flour

1 teaspoon baking powder

$\frac{1}{4}$ teaspoon salt

4 eggs, separated

$\frac{3}{4}$ cup sugar

$\frac{1}{2}$ teaspoon almond extract

2 tablespoons water

Raspberry jam

Custard

3 cups milk

$\frac{1}{3}$ cup sugar

$1\frac{1}{2}$ tablespoons flour

5 egg yolks

1 teaspoon vanilla

Sponge Cake Directions

1. Preheat oven to 375°.

2. Sift together flour, baking powder, and salt.

3. Beat egg whites until stiff, gradually adding 1/2 cup of the sugar.

4. In a separate bowl, beat yolks until thick, gradually adding remaining sugar.

5. Add almond extract to yolks.

6. Add water gradually, while beating.

7. Fold in egg whites.

8. Sift flour mixture, 1/3 at a time, over the mixture, folding in each time.

9. Turn into parchment paper-lined jelly roll pan and bake 18 minutes.

10. Cool on rack.

11. Slice in half; spread raspberry jam over one half and place other half on top.

12. Cut into 1-inch cubes.

Custard Directions

1. Heat milk in top of double boiler.

2. Mix sugar and flour together in separate bowl.

3. Add yolks to flour mix, blend well.

4. Add milk, stirring with whisk.

5. Return to double boiler and cook over simmering water, stirring constantly until thick.

6. Cool quickly by placing pan in cold water.

7. Strain.

8. Add vanilla and chill.

Filling Directions & Ingredients

Sweet sherry

Use any combination of the following fruits:

Cherries pitted and cut in half;

Peaches or nectarines peeled; and thinly sliced

berries— blueberries, raspberries, blackberries, strawberries

Whipped cream

To assemble

1. Arrange sponge cake cubes in bottom of deep-sided bowl (preferably glass trifle bowl).

2. Pour sherry over, enough to moisten, but not to make it soggy.

3. Layer with fruit.

4. Pour custard over all and top with whipped cream.

Blackberry Sauce

Ingredients

$\frac{1}{2}$ cup water

$\frac{1}{2}$ cup sugar

$\frac{1}{2}$ cup dry red wine

3 tablespoons lemon juice

$1\frac{1}{2}$ tablespoons cornstarch

1 cup blackberries

$\frac{1}{4}$ teaspoon cinnamon

Directions

1. Combine water, sugar, wine, lemon juice, and cornstarch in medium saucepan. Cook over medium heat until mixture boils.

2. Add berries; boil until sauce thickens enough to coat back of spoon, stirring constantly, about 5 minutes.

3. Cool; stir in cinnamon

Great on pancakes or ice cream.

Peach Blackberry Crisp

Serves 8 to 10

Ingredients

32 ounces peaches, sliced

12 ounces blackberries, whole

6 ounces granulated sugar

2 lemons, zest and juice

20 ounces of streusel

Streusel - Ingredients

8 ounces butter

4 ounces granulated sugar

8 ounces flour

Ground cinnamon to taste

Streusel Directions

1. Cut butter into sugar and flour until crumbly (walnut size pieces).

2. Flavor with cinnamon.

Directions

1. Preheat oven to 400°.

2. Place peaches and blackberries in greased pan.

3. Add sugar and lemon.

4. Mix to distribute evenly.

5. Top with streusel.

6. Bake at 400° for 24 minutes or until crisp is brown and bubbly.

Fresh Raspberry Mousse
with Shaved Chocolate and Chambord

Serves 4

Ingredients

2 cups fresh raspberries

$\frac{1}{2}$ cup sugar

$\frac{1}{2}$ cup water

4 egg yolks

1$\frac{1}{2}$ cups heavy cream

1 teaspoon pure vanilla extract

2 ounces milk chocolate

2 ounces dark chocolate

2 ounces white chocolate

4 sprigs of mint

4 lady fingers or similar cookies

4 ounces Chambord

Directions

1. Start by blending the raspberries, water, and sugar in a mixer or Cuisinart until smooth.

2. Strain the liquid through a sieve into a stainless mixing bowl to remove the seeds.

3. Make a custard by adding the egg yolks to the mixture and using the bowl as a double boiler on top of a gently boiling pot on the stove. Stir the mixture frequently as it cooks, for about 20 minutes or until it is the consistency of yogurt. Place in cooler to chill.

4. Make whipped cream out of the heavy cream and vanilla. Set aside 1/2 cup to use later as garnish.

5. Fold the whipped cream into the chilled custard to form the mousse and pour into parfait glasses or decorative bowls and chill to let set up (approximately 2 hours).

6. Shave or grate the three chocolates over the mousse.

7. Garnish with the lady fingers, mint, and remaining whipped cream; pour 1 ounce of Chambord over each just prior to serving.

Frozen Chocolate Amaretto Ice Cream Pie

Serves 8

Ingredients

Pie Crust

- 2 cups graham cracker crumbs
- $\frac{1}{2}$ cup cocoa
- $\frac{1}{4}$ cup coconut flakes
- $\frac{1}{4}$ cup chopped pecans
- $\frac{1}{2}$ cup melted butter or magarine

Pie Filling

- 1 quart chocolate ice cream
- $\frac{1}{4}$ cup Amaretto

Directions

Pie Crust

1. Preheat oven to 350°.
2. Mix all ingredients and press into a 10-inch pie pan.
3. Bake at 350° for 10 minutes. Remove from oven and let cool.

Pie Filling

1. Soften the ice cream and add the Amaretto.
2. Fill pie shell with the ice cream mixture. Place in freezer until frozen.

Slice and serve with fresh whipped cream. Your favorite cordial may be substituted for the Amaretto.

Blueberry Buckle

Serves 12

Ingredients

$\frac{3}{4}$ cup sugar

$\frac{1}{4}$ cup shortening

1 egg

$\frac{1}{2}$ cup milk

2 cups flour

$\frac{1}{2}$ teaspoons salt

2 teaspoons baking powder

2 cups blueberries

Topping

$\frac{1}{2}$ cup sugar

$\frac{1}{3}$ cup flour

$\frac{1}{4}$ cup butter

1 teaspoon cinnamon

Directions

1. Preheat oven to 350°.

2. Beat together sugar, shortening, and eggs; add milk and blend.

3. Sift flour, salt, and baking powder into batter and blend; add berries.

4. Pour into a greased 8x8-inch pan.

5. For the topping, blend sugar, flour, butter, and cinnamon; crumble on top of batter.

6. Bake at 350° for 60 minutes.

Fudgy Orange-Zucchini Cake

Ingredients

$2\frac{1}{2}$ cups flour

$\frac{1}{2}$ cup cocoa

$2\frac{1}{2}$ teaspoons baking powder

$1\frac{1}{2}$ teaspoons baking soda

1 teaspoon salt

1 teaspoon cinnamon

$\frac{3}{4}$ cup butter

2 cups sugar

3 eggs, slightly beaten

2 teaspoons vanilla

$\frac{1}{2}$ cup milk

3 cups grated zucchini

Grated zest of 1 orange

1 cup chopped nuts

Powdered sugar

Directions

1. Preheat oven to 350°.

2. Grease and flour a bundt or angel food pan.

3. Sift flour, baking powder, baking soda, salt, and cinnamon together.

4. In a separate bowl, cream butter and sugar until fluffy.

5. Add eggs, vanilla, and milk to butter mixture.

6. Stir in dry ingredients until well blended.

7. Fold in zucchini, orange zest, and nuts.

8. Bake 50 to 60 minutes.

9. Cool for 15 minutes before turning onto rack to cool thoroughly.

10. Dust with powdered sugar.

Optional Glaze

$1\frac{1}{4}$ cups sifted confectioners' sugar

$\frac{1}{4}$ cup fresh orange juice

1 teaspoon vanilla

Directions

1. Mix all ingredients until sugar is dissolved.

2. Drizzle over cooled cake.

Chocolate Marvel Pie

Serves 8

Ingredients

1 baked pie shell

1 6-ounce package of semi-sweet chocolate bits

2 tablespoons sugar

3 tablespoons milk

4 egg yolks

1 teaspoon vanilla

4 egg whites

Directions

1. Melt chocolate bits, sugar and milk in saucepan.

2. Cool.

3. Beat in egg yolks one at a time; add the vanilla.

4. Beat egg whites in separate bowl until stiff.

5. Fold egg whites into chocolate-egg yolk mixture.

6. Pour into cooled baked pie shell.

Macedonia Fruit Salad

Serves 4

Ingredients

1 melon

1 peach

1 kiwi

1 plum

4 strawberries

12 raspberries

12 blueberries

1 banana, sliced in wheels

1 cloister of grapes, white seedless

1 mango

4 ounces of Sambuca Romana

$\frac{1}{4}$ cup coarse sugar

Directions

1. Slice and dice all fruit, add 2 ounces of fresh lemon juice, Sambuca, and sugar. Mix well.

2. Chill for 1 hour and serve with whipped cream.

Raspberry Cream Cheese Coffee Cake

Serves 10

Ingredients

Cake and Topping

2$\frac{1}{2}$ cups all-purpose flour

$\frac{3}{4}$ cup of sugar

12 tablespoons butter - 1$\frac{1}{2}$ sticks

$\frac{1}{2}$ teaspoon baking powder

$\frac{1}{2}$ teaspoon baking soda

$\frac{1}{4}$ teaspoon salt

$\frac{3}{4}$ cup of sour cream

1 egg, slightly beaten

1 teaspoon almond extract

$\frac{1}{2}$ cup sliced almonds

Filling

1 8-ounce package of cream cheese, softened

$\frac{1}{4}$ cup sugar

1 egg

$\frac{1}{2}$ cup raspberry jam

Directions

1. Preheat oven to 350°.

2. Grease and flour a 9-inch spring form pan.

3. Combine flour and sugar; cut in the butter until mixture resembles crumbs.

4. Reserve 1 cup of the crumbs for the topping.

5. To the remaining crumb mixture add baking powder, baking soda, salt, sour cream, egg, and almond extract. Blend well.

6. Spread dough over bottom and 2 inches up the sides of the prepared spring form pan. Dough should be 1/2-inch thick on all sides.

7. Combine together cream cheese, sugar, and egg; spread evenly over the dough in the pan.

8. Spread jam over the cheese filling. The jam may need to be warmed to make it easier to spread.

9. In small bowl combine 1 cup of the reserved crumb mixture and the almonds; sprinkle over top.

10. Bake 60 to 90 minutes or until cream cheese filling is set and the crust is golden brown.

11. Cool in pan for 15 minutes. Remove sides of pan; serve warm or cool.

12. Cover and refrigerate leftovers.

Lemon Squares

Makes 16

Ingredients

Bottom Layer

1 cup flour

$\frac{1}{2}$ cup confectioners' sugar

$\frac{1}{2}$ cup butter, softened

Top Layer

1 cup sugar

2 tablespoons flour

$\frac{1}{2}$ teaspoon baking powder

2 eggs, beaten

3 tablespoons lemon juice

1 teaspoon confectioners' sugar

Directions

1. Preheat oven to 325°.

2. Blend bottom layer ingredients until crumbly and press flat and evenly into a greased 8x12-inch pan.

3. Bake for 15 minutes.

4. Mix first 3 top layer ingredients together in food processor.

5. Add eggs and lemon juice and pour over crust.

6. Bake for 25 minutes.

7. Cool a little and dust with confectioners' sugar.

8. Cut into squares.

Raspberry Pie

Serves 8

Ingredients

- 1 pie crust
- 1 cup sugar
- 2 tablespoons cornstarch
- 1 dash salt
- $1\frac{1}{2}$ tablespoons tapioca
- 6 cups raspberries (use whole frozen, not in juice)
- 2 tablespoons butter
- 1 tablespoon of heavy cream (optional)

Directions

1. Preheat oven to 375°.
2. Combine sugar, cornstarch, salt, and tapioca.
3. Mix in berries to coat.
4. Place in pie crust. Dot pie with 2 tablespoon of butter.
5. Put top crust on and rub with heavy cream.
6. Put foil around edge of crust.
7. Bake until golden, about 45 minutes.

Pumpkin Bread

Serves 6 to 8

Ingredients

$\frac{2}{3}$ cup shortening

$2\frac{2}{3}$ cups sugar

4 eggs

1 pound can pumpkin

$\frac{2}{3}$ cup water

$3\frac{1}{3}$ cups flour

2 teaspoons baking soda

$1\frac{1}{2}$ teaspoons salt

$\frac{1}{2}$ teaspoon baking powder

1 teaspoon cinnamon

1 teaspoon cloves

$\frac{2}{3}$ cup chopped nuts

$\frac{2}{3}$ cup raisins

Directions

1. Preheat over to 350°.

2. In a large bowl, cream together shortening and sugar until fluffy.

3. Stir in eggs, pumpkin, and water.

4. Blend in flour, soda, salt, baking powder, cinnamon, and cloves.

5. Stir in nuts and raisins.

6. Pour into 2 greased loaf pans and bake at 350° for about 70 minutes.

Sour Cream Coffee Cake

Serves 10

Ingredients

Cake

$\frac{1}{4}$ pound butter

1 cup sugar

2 eggs

1 cup sour cream

1 teaspoon baking soda

$1\frac{1}{2}$ cups flour

$\frac{1}{2}$ teaspoon baking powder

1 teaspoon vanilla

Filling

$\frac{1}{4}$ cup sugar

2 tablespoons walnuts, chopped

1 tablespoon cinnamon

Directions

1. Preheat oven to 350°.

2. Cream together butter, sugar, and eggs.

3. Combine sour cream and baking soda in a separate bowl and add to creamed mixture.

4. Add flour, baking powder, and vanilla and blend well.

5. Pour 1/2 mixture into a greased tube pan.

6. Add 1/2 of the filling mixture.

7. Add rest of the batter, followed by the rest of the filling mixture.

8. Bake for 45 minutes.

Hearty Granola

Ingredients

1 cup canola oil

1 cup honey

6 cups oats

1 cup sunflower seeds

$\frac{1}{2}$ cup sesame seeds

2 cups almonds, pecans, or walnuts

Directions

1. Preheat oven to 250°.

2. Combine oil and honey in pan and heat until warm.

3. Combine oats, sunflower seeds, sesame seeds, and nuts in a bowl and pour oil/honey mixture over all. Mix thoroughly.

4. Spread onto sheet pans in thin layers.

5. Bake for 2 to 3 hours at 250°, stirring occasionally.

6. Test for doneness by removing and cooling a small spoonful.

7. Cool completely on sheet pans.

Dried fruits may be added if desired—banana chips, raisins, dried cherries, dried cranberries, dried apples, or dried apricots.

Wild Mushroom Tart

Serves 12 as an appetizer

Ingredients

Crust

- 1⅓ cups all-purpose flour
- ¼ teaspoon salt
- ½ cup unsalted chilled butter, diced
- 5 tablespoons or more ice water

Filling

- 2 cups hot water
- 2 ounces dried porcini mushrooms
- 3 tablespoons butter
- 1 cup finely chopped onions
- ¼ cup finely chopped Italian parsley
- 1½ teaspoons chopped fresh thyme or 1 teaspoon dried
- 1½ teaspoons chopped fresh rosemary or 1 teaspoon dried
- 1 tablespoon tomato paste
- 1 tablespoon Cognac or Brandy
- ¾ cup Parmesan cheese
- 2 eggs beaten
- Salt and pepper to taste

Directions

Crust

1. Combine flour and salt in processor. Add butter and cut in until mixture resembles coarse meal.

2. Add 5 tablespoons of water; process until moist clumps form, adding more water by teaspoonfuls if dough is dry.

3. Gather dough into ball and flatten into disk, wrap in plastic and refrigerate until firm (about 1 hour).

Filling

1. Combine water and mushrooms in medium bowl and let stand until mushrooms soften, about 40 minutes.

2. Drain mushrooms, reserve 1½ cups of soaking liquid. Coarsely chop mushrooms.

3. Melt butter in skillet; add onion, parsley, chopped herbs, and chopped mushrooms; sauté until onion is soft.

4. Mix in tomato paste and Cognac; slowly pour in reserved mushroom liquid, leaving sediment in bowl.

5. Boil until liquid evaporates, stirring occasionally, about 15 minutes.

6. Mix in Parmesan cheese, season with salt and pepper, and mix in eggs.

The dough and filling can be prepared one day ahead and refrigerated.

1. Preheat oven to 375°.

2. Roll out dough on lightly floured surface to 14-inch round. Transfer to 11-inch tart pan with removable bottom. Press dough gently into pan and trim excess dough.

3. Freeze for 15 minutes.

4. Line crust with foil and pie weights or dried beans. Bake until sides of crust are set, about 20 minutes.

5. Remove foil and weights and continue to bake until crust is golden, piercing with toothpick if crust bubbles, about 25 minutes.

6. Cool crust completely.

7. Spread filling in crust and bake until filling is set, about 25 minutes.

8. Garnish with thyme or rosemary sprigs.

Meal in a Muffin

Serves 10

Ingredients

1 medium carrot, peeled

1 large Granny Smith apple, cored

$\frac{1}{2}$ cup vegetable oil

2 large eggs

$\frac{1}{3}$ cup sugar

2 teaspoons vanilla

$\frac{1}{3}$ cup unsweetened, shredded coconut

$\frac{1}{3}$ cup raisins

$\frac{1}{3}$ cup pecan halves

$\frac{3}{4}$ cup whole wheat flour

$\frac{1}{2}$ cup old-fashioned rolled oats

3 tablespoons wheat germ

1 teaspoon baking soda

$\frac{3}{4}$ teaspoon ground cinnamon

$\frac{1}{2}$ teaspoon baking powder

$\frac{1}{4}$ teaspoon salt

$\frac{1}{4}$ teaspoon ground ginger

$\frac{1}{4}$ teaspoon freshly grated nutmeg

Directions

1. Preheat oven to 375°.

2. Shred carrot and apple with medium shredding disc of Cuisinart. Set aside.

3. Process oil, eggs, sugar, and vanilla with metal blade for about 30 seconds.

4. Scrape down; add carrots and apple and remaining ingredients.

5. Pulse 6 to 8 times. Don't over process.

6. Fill muffin cups 3/4 full.

7. Bake about 20 minutes.

Apple Bran Muffin

Serves 10

Ingredients

- 2 cups green apples, peeled, cored and finely diced
- 1 teaspoon cinnamon
- $\frac{1}{4}$ cup apple juice
- Juice of $\frac{1}{2}$ lemon
- $\frac{1}{4}$ cup brown sugar
- 1 cup Quaker unprocessed bran
- $\frac{1}{2}$ cup King Arthur stoneground whole wheat flour
- 1 teaspoon baking soda
- 2 tablespoons corn oil
- 1 egg, slightly whipped

Directions

1. Heat a teflon pan and sauté the first four ingredients until apples are tender, approximately 2 to 4 minutes.

2. Pour into a bowl and let cool, then add remaining ingredients and mix until smooth. Do not overmix.

3. Spray muffin pan with 100% vegetable oil and spoon 1 1/2 ounces of batter or 4 tablespoons into each cup.

4. Bake at 325° for 30 to 35 minutes.

Carrot Bran Muffin

Serves 10

Ingredients

- $\frac{1}{2}$ cup carrot, shredded
- $\frac{1}{2}$ cup King Arthur stoneground whole wheat Flour
- $1\frac{1}{4}$ cup Quaker unprocessed bran
- 1 teaspoon baking soda
- 1 teaspoon cinnamon
- $\frac{1}{4}$ cup brown sugar
- 1 egg white
- 2 teaspoons corn oil
- 1 cup carrot juice

Directions

1. Combine first six ingredients and mix.

2. In a separate bowl, lightly whip egg white, add remaining ingredients and mix.

3. Add egg mixture to dry ingredients and blend until smooth, being careful not to overmix and toughen the muffins.

4. Spray muffin pan with 100% vegetable oil and spoon 1 1/2 ounces of batter or 4 tablespoons into each cup.

5. Bake at 350° for 30 to 35 minutes.

Salad of Grilled Venison, Peaches, Raspberries, and Young Greens

Serves 4

Ingredients

1 pound boneless venison steak or loin medallion

1 fresh peach

$\frac{1}{2}$ pint fresh raspberries

4 large handfuls mesclun or 2 bunches watercress

$\frac{1}{4}$ cup grapeseed oil (substitute peanut or canola oil, if necessary)

1 ounce raspberry vinegar

1 small shallot, minced

1 teaspoon Dijon mustard

Salt and pepper to taste

Directions

1. Coat the venison steak in black pepper and set aside.

2. Clean the greens and place in a bowl.

3. Mix the oil, vinegar, shallot, and mustard. Taste for seasoning.

4. Heat a large, heavy skillet until very hot. Add a little oil and place the venison carefully in pan. Sear well on both sides. Turn down heat and cook until meat is just firm, about 4 minutes per side. Let rest.

5. Slice the peach.

6. Toss the greens with the dressing and set on a large platter. Arrange the peaches and raspberries around the outer area of the platter.

7. Slice the venison on the bias and place in the center. Serve immediately.

Crostini al Portobello

Serves 4

Ingredients

$\frac{1}{2}$ pound portobello mushrooms

1 shallot

8 slices country bread, 1-inch thick

2 ounces marsala wine

2 ounces extra-virgin olive oil

8 shavings Pecorino romano cheese

Directions

1. Sauté oil and shallot.

2. Add mushrooms, marsala wine; burn off alcohol and reduce.

3. Top over grilled bread.

Apple Cider Salad Dressing

Serves 6

Ingredients

$\frac{1}{3}$ cup unsweetened apple cider

2 tablespoons fresh lemon juice

2 tablespoons cider vinegar

1 tablespoon vegetable oil

1 teaspoon Dijon mustard

$\frac{1}{8}$ teaspoon salt

$\frac{1}{4}$ teaspoon pepper

$\frac{1}{8}$ teaspoon cinnamon

Directions

Whisk all the ingredients together and serve on greens such as red leaf or bib lettuce.

Cabot Cheddar Cheese Dressing

Ingredients

2 cups mayonnaise

4 ounces Cabot feta cheese

Balsamic vinegar

Fresh lemon juice

Dry mustard

White pepper

Horseradish

4 ounces Cabot garlic dill cheddar cheese, grated

4 ounces Cabot Cottage Cheese

4 ounces Cabot sour cream

Olive oil

2 tablespoons parsley, chopped

$\frac{1}{4}$ teaspoon paprika

$\frac{1}{2}$ teaspoon Worcestershire sauce

Pinch of garlic powder or 1 garlic clove minced

Directions

1. Blend mayonnaise, cottage cheese, feta, and sour cream

2. Whip in oil alternately with lemon juice.

3. Add remaining ingredients. Chill before serving.

Fresh Broccoli Salad

Serves 6 to 8

Ingredients

- 1 head broccoli, chopped
- 1 cup sunflower seeds
- 1 cup raisins
- $\frac{1}{2}$ cup walnuts, chopped
- 1 small, 4-ounce red onion, diced

Directions

1. Mix first 5 ingredients together.
2. Blend dressing ingredients.
3. Pour dressing over salad and toss.

Dressing:

- 1 cup mayonnaise
- $\frac{1}{4}$ cup sugar
- 2 tablespoons red wine vinegar

Carrot Salad

Serves 12 (one-half cup serving)

Ingredients

2 cups raisins

2 cups grated carrots

2 cups chopped walnuts

Directions

1. Mix top three ingredients together, for the salad mixture, and set aside.

2. Combine all ingredients for dressing and mix thoroughly. Add the dressing mixture, to taste, to the salad.

Dressing Ingredients

8 ounces Cabot plain no fat yogurt

$\frac{1}{4}$ cup of honey

$\frac{1}{4}$ teaspoon ground nutmeg

$\frac{1}{2}$ teaspoon of vanilla extract

1 teaspoon ground cinnamon

Endive Salad

Serves 6

Ingredients

- 6 endive, sliced diagonally
- 3 medium red apples, unpeeled, cored and cut into chunks
- $\frac{1}{2}$ cup walnut halves
- $\frac{1}{2}$ cup currants, soaked in warm water 30 minutes
- $\frac{1}{2}$ cup canola oil
- 2 tablespoons cider vinegar or raspberry vinegar
- 1 tablespoon cream

Directions

1. Toss together endive, apples, walnuts, and currants in large bowl.

2. Mix oil and vinegar together in another bowl. Add cream.

3. Pour liquid mixture over salad just before serving.

Spicy Clam Chowder

Serves 4

Ingredients

- 4 slices of bacon
- 2 medium onions, finely chopped (approximately 2 cups)
- 1 small can of diced green chilies (7 ounces)
- 2 cloves of garlic, minced
- $\frac{1}{2}$ teaspoon ground cumin
- 1 medium-size thin-skin potato, diced, approximately 1 cup
- 2 10-ounce cans of whole baby clams; drain and reserve the clam juice
- 1 quart of whole milk

Condiments

Sour cream

Green or red chili salsa

Tortilla or corn chips

Directions

1. In 4 or 5-quart pot, cook bacon over medium heat until crisp; drain, crumble and set aside. Reserve drippings in pan.

2. Add onions, chilies, garlic, and cumin to drippings. Cook about 5 minutes over low heat, stirring, until onions are soft.

3. Add reserved clam juice and potatoes to onion mixture. Bring to a soft boil; cover and boil gently until potatoes are tender, approximately 20 minutes.

4. Add milk and drained clams; heat, stirring occasionally until hot. Do not boil.

5. Serve bacon and condiments in separate bowl.

Cauliflower Soup with Mushrooms

Serves 6

Ingredients

- 1 large onion, chopped
- 2 tablespoons olive oil
- 1 tablespoon butter
- 2 cloves of garlic, minced
- 1 head of cauliflower, chopped or broken into small pieces
- 5 cups chicken stock
- 2 tablespoons thyme, separated
- 1 cup white wine
- $\frac{1}{2}$ teaspoon salt
- $\frac{1}{4}$ teaspoon pepper
- 1 tablespoon butter
- 2 shallots, chopped
- $1\frac{1}{2}$ cups mushrooms, sliced – we suggest wild mushrooms
- 6 tablespoons plain yogurt – reserve for garnish
- 2 tablespoons fresh parsley, chopped – reserve for garnish

Directions

1. Sauté onions in olive oil and butter until translucent, then add garlic. Cook 2 to 3 minutes; keep stirring. making sure the garlic does not burn.

2. Add cauliflower and stir to mix ingredients together. Add chicken stock, 1 tablespoon of thyme, and wine. Bring to boil, then lower heat and simmer until cauliflower is soft, about 15 to 20 minutes. Add salt and pepper and remove from heat. Let cool.

3. Sauté the shallots in 1 tablespoon of butter until translucent, then add mushrooms and sauté until the mushrooms are golden brown. Set aside.

4. Take cooled soup mixture and purée.

5. Return to stock pot and bring to boil, turn heat down and simmer uncovered for 15 minutes until liquid reduces. Add 1 tablespoon of thyme and the mushroom and shallot mixture. Simmer for 5 more minutes.

6. Serve in individual soup bowls with a garnish of 1 tablespoon of yogurt and sprinkle parsley on top.

Curried Pea Soup

Serves 8

Ingredients

$1\frac{2}{3}$ cups zucchini, washed and chopped

$1\frac{1}{3}$ cups onions, chopped

$\frac{1}{3}$ cup celery, chopped

1 green apple, peeled, cored, and chopped

2 cups green peas, frozen

2 cups chicken stock

2 cloves of garlic

1 teaspoon curry powder

1 teaspoon salt (optional)

$\frac{1}{4}$ teaspoon white pepper

Directions

1. Combine all the ingredients in a heavy-bottom sauce pot. Place over high heat and bring to a boil.

2. Reduce heat and simmer over medium heat for 20 minutes.

3. Remove from heat; place in blender and purée until smooth.

4. Return to pot and heat before serving. Garnish with fresh parsley.

Butternut Squash Soup

Serves 6

Ingredients

3 cups butternut squash, peeled, deseeded, and chopped

1 cup onions, diced

$1\frac{1}{4}$ cup green apple, peeled, cored and chopped

$2\frac{1}{2}$ cups chicken stock

$\frac{1}{2}$ teaspoon salt

White pepper to taste

Sliced scallions or chopped parsley, reserve for garnish

Directions

1. Combine all ingredients in a saucepan, cover and simmer over medium heat for 20 to 30 minutes.

2. Remove sachet bag; pour mixture into a blender and process until smooth.

3. Heat six bowls in 150° oven.

4. Place 3/4 cup of soup in each. Garnish with sliced scallions or chopped parsley.

Sachet Bag:

1 bay leaf

1 sprig fresh rosemary

2 sprigs fresh thyme

1 clove garlic

German Potato Salad

Serves 6 to 8

Ingredients

4 cups of boiled potatoes, sliced

$\frac{1}{4}$ pound bacon, cut in pieces

1 medium onion, sliced fine

1 teaspoon salt

1 teaspoon sugar

1 teaspoon flour

1 teaspoon dry mustard

$\frac{1}{8}$ teaspoon pepper

$\frac{1}{2}$ cup vinegar

$\frac{1}{2}$ cup water

May be made ahead and reheated.

Directions

1. Preheat oven to 350°.

2. Boil potatoes; slice and place in casserole dish.

3. Fry bacon until light brown. Remove bacon from fat and put with potatoes.

4. Fry onion in fat until transparent and add to potatoes.

5. Add salt, sugar, flour, pepper, and mustard to fat and mix quickly. Add vinegar and water and bring to a boil.

6. Pour over potatoes and mix thoroughly.

7. Bake at 350° for 30 minutes.

Roasted Pepper and Eggplant Terrine

Serves 20 as appetizer; 10 as main course

Ingredients

6 ounces balsamic vinaigrette, mixed with plenty of fresh basil, chopped

1 tablespoon granulated gelatin

$1\frac{1}{4}$ pounds small eggplants, sliced and grilled

$1\frac{1}{4}$ pounds bell peppers, roasted and julienned

Directions

1. Line a terrine mold (or 1 1/2 pound loaf plan) with plastic wrap.

2. Sprinkle the gelatin over the surface of the vinaigrette and allow it to soften. Warm the vinaigrette gently to melt the gelatin crystals.

3. Fill the mold by alternating layers of eggplant, roasted peppers, and the vinaigrette/gelatin mix.

4. Cover the terrine with plastic wrap and weight the terrine.

5. Refrigerate overnight until completely firm.

To grill eggplant

Lightly salt and pepper the eggplant slices, brush with olive oil, and grill.

To roast peppers

Slice peppers in half; remove seeds. Broil skin side up, 3 to 4 inches from flame until charred. Place in plastic bag, twist tie the bag and allow peppers to steam for about 15 minutes. Remove peppers from bag and skins with slip off.

Note: Can be served with a side of mixed greens tossed in the same vinaigrette and croutons. Croutons should be made by thinly slicing a baguette; brush each slice with olive oil, rub with a clove of garlic, dust lightly with Parmesan cheese and brown under a broiler.

Sweet-and-Sour Braised Red Cabbage

Serves 4

Ingredients

½ cup raspberry vinegar

3 tablespoons packed dark brown sugar

1 cup chicken stock

1 teaspoon caraway seeds

2 pounds of red cabbage, shredded

Salt and pepper to taste

Directions

1. Combine all ingredients in large kettle and bring to a boil.

2. Simmer, covered for 50 minutes or until just tender.

3. Remove lid and boil until liquid has almost evaporated.

Green Mountain Inn Chicken

*Breaded chicken breast stuffed with apples and cheddar,
served with an apple cider black currant sauce.*

Serves 4

Ingredients

- 4 6-ounce large boneless chicken breasts
- 1 large Macintosh apple, cored and sliced
- 4 slices sharp Cabot cheddar cheese
- 2 eggs beaten
- $\frac{1}{2}$ cup flour
- $1\frac{1}{2}$ cups bread crumbs
- $\frac{1}{4}$ cup drawn butter

Sauce

- $\frac{1}{2}$ cup cider
- $\frac{1}{2}$ cup chicken stock
- $\frac{1}{2}$ cup Creme de Cassis
- $\frac{1}{4}$ cup black currants
- 2 teaspoons cornstarch
- $\frac{1}{3}$ cup water
- $\frac{1}{4}$ teaspoon salt
- $\frac{1}{8}$ teaspoon pepper

Suggested Wine

*Cabernet Sauvignon
Red Bordeaux*

Directions

1. Preheat oven to 375°.

2. Make the sauce by bringing the cider, chicken stock, Cassis, and black currants to a boil in a medium saucepan, then reducing the heat to let simmer for five minutes. Thicken the sauce with the cornstarch and water mixture. Add salt and pepper and set aside to be reheated for service.

3. Make a pocket in the middle of the chicken breast by cutting horizontally along the middle of the chicken breast, but not completely through the opposite side or either end of the breast.

4. Place two or three of the apple slices and a slice of cheddar in the fold created.

5. Roll the stuffed chicken breast in the flour then dip into the beaten eggs and roll in the bread crumbs to bread the chicken.

6. Heat on stove in ovenproof sauté pan over high heat until hot. Add drawn butter to the pan, followed by the chicken breasts.

7. Brown on one side; turn the breasts and place pan in oven for 8 to 10 minutes or until chicken is fully cooked.

8. Slice the chicken and fan out on the plate. Top with the sauce and serve.

Stuffed Whisky Pork Loin

Serves 6

Ingredients

$\frac{3}{4}$ cup mixed whole dried fruit

$\frac{1}{4}$ cup mixed chopped dried fruit

$\frac{1}{2}$ cup whisky

2 pounds boned pork loin

$\frac{1}{2}$ cup heavy cream

2 tablespoons of demi glace

Salt

Pepper

Caraway seeds – optional

Directions

1. Marinate both fruits in whisky in separate bowls for 2 hours. Drain and reserve liquid.

2. Preheat oven to 350°.

3. Stuff whole fruit into center of pork loin. Season outside of pork with salt, pepper, and caraway seeds. Tie the pork loin with butchers' twine.

4. Sear in heavy pan on all sides, then transfer to a preheated 350° oven and roast for 1 to 1 1/2 hours or until a meat thermometer registers 160° F.

5. Remove from pan and let rest 15 minutes.

6. Place chopped dried fruit in a sauté pan; add 3 tablespoons of reserved whisky and flame until extinguished. Add heavy cream and reduce to sauce consistency. Add 2 tablespoons of demi glace and whisk until incorporated.

7. Slice pork loin and serve with sauce.

Suggested Wine

Red Zinfandel
Syrah

Cornish Game Hens Stuffed with Wild Rice

Serves 6

Ingredients

- 6 Rock Cornish game hens
- 1 cup wild rice
- $2\frac{1}{2}$ cups chicken broth
- 6 tablespoons of butter – reserve 3 tablespoons
- 1 cup chopped onions
- $\frac{1}{4}$ pound of mushrooms, chopped
- $\frac{1}{2}$ tablespoon Worcestershire sauce
- $\frac{1}{2}$ teaspoon freshly ground black pepper
- 2 teaspoons of salt
- 1 teaspoon of paprika
- 12 small white onions
- 1 cup dry white wine
- 2 tablespoons cognac

Directions

1. Preheat oven to 350°.

2. Wash rice well and drain. Combine in saucepan with broth; bring to boil, cover, reduce heat to low, and cook for 20 minutes.

3. Drain off any remaining liquid.

4. Melt 3 tablespoons of butter in skillet and sauté onions and mushrooms for 10 minutes.

5. Add wild rice, Worcestershire sauce and 1/4 teaspoon of pepper to the onion and mushroom mixture.

6. Fill the hens with the rice. Sew or skewer the openings of the hens and season the outside with salt, paprika and the remaining pepper.

7. Melt 3 tablespoons of butter in a shallow roasting pan and brown the birds and onions over medium heat. Add wine to pan and roast in 350° oven 60 to 90 minutes, basting frequently until tender.

8. Make pan gravy to serve on the side.

Arrange hens on a serving dish. Heat cognac and pour over.

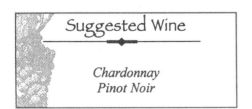

Suggested Wine

Chardonnay
Pinot Noir

Poached Halibut with Sauce Duglere

Serves 6

Ingredients

- 3 pounds halibut
- 3 cups of dry white wine
- 1 medium onion, chopped (approximately 8 ounces)
- 8 ounces sliced mushrooms
- 4 tablespoons of butter
- 1 ounce of flour
- 1 cup heavy cream
- 14 ounces canned tomatoes, peeled, diced, and drained
- 2 tablespoons of fresh chopped parsley
- $\frac{1}{4}$ teaspoon salt
- $\frac{1}{8}$ teaspoon pepper

Directions

1. Place fish in a saucepan, cover with white wine, bring to boil, reduce heat, and simmer 8 minutes.

2. Sauté onions and mushrooms with 2 tablespoons of butter in large saucepan.

3. In a bowl mix remaining 2 tablespoons of butter (melted) and flour until smooth.

4. Remove fish from stock and keep warm.

5. Add stock to onions and mushrooms; add flour and butter mixture and simmer; stir until thickened.

6. Add cream, tomatoes, and parsley and stir until smooth consistency.

7. Season with salt and pepper to taste.

8. Add more wine or cream if sauce is too thick.

9. Cover hot halibut with sauce; serve immediately.

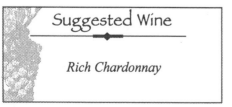

Suggested Wine

Rich Chardonnay

Baked Rainbow Trout with Portobello Mushroom and Spinach Stuffing

Serves 6

Ingredients

6 8-ounce rainbow trouts

Lemon juice, butter, and paprika to coat each fish

Stuffing

2 teaspoons of garlic, chopped

1 large onion, diced (approximately 12 ounces)

4 ribs of celery, diced

3 tablespoons margarine

2 pounds portobello mushrooms, washed and diced

$1\frac{1}{2}$ pounds fresh spinach, washed and chopped

1 teaspoon chervil

$\frac{1}{2}$ teaspoon salt

$\frac{1}{2}$ teaspoon onion powder

$1\frac{1}{2}$ cups Ritz Cracker crumbs

Directions

Preheat oven to 400°.

For Stuffing

1. Combine the garlic, onion, celery, and margarine in saucepan; cook for 5 minutes in medium-high heat.

2. Add the portobello mushrooms; cook 2 to 3 minutes.

3. Add the spinach, chervil, onion powder, and salt; cook about 2 minutes, until the spinach is wilted but not mushy. Remove from heat.

4. Stir in the Ritz Cracker crumbs.

To Prepare Trout

1. Fill the inside of a whole rainbow trout with stuffing mixture.

2. Place trout on a buttered 8x11-inch baking dish.

3. Coat trout with lemon juice; butter and sprinkle with paprika.

4. Bake in 1/4-inch of water for 15 to 20 minutes.

Suggested Wine

Dry Riesling
Pinot Gris (Grigio)

Pasta alla Puttanesca con Vongole

Serves 6

Ingredients

- $\frac{1}{4}$ cup olive oil

- 1 tablespoon finely minced garlic

- 2 12-ounce cans crushed tomatoes or 4 cups peeled, chopped, fresh tomatoes

- $\frac{1}{3}$ cup finely chopped parsley

- 2 tablespoons finely chopped fresh basil or 1 tablespoon dried

- 2 tablespoons finely chopped oregano or 1 tablespoon dried

- $\frac{1}{2}$ tablespoon red pepper flakes

- 1 3-ounce bottle capers

- 1 can of pitted imported black olives

- 2 2-ounce cans anchovies

- 2 dozen mussels

- 1 pound of pasta

Directions

1. Heat oil over low heat, add garlic and sauté. Then add anchovies and mash to make a paste.

2. Add the tomatoes and half the parsley, the basil, oregano, pepper, capers, and the olives. Cook over medium heat for 20 minutes, stirring frequently.

3. Add the mussels and the reserved parsley. Cover the skillet or pan and cook for about 5 minutes or until all the mussels are open.

4. Serve over pasta.

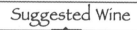

Suggested Wine

Pinot Grigio
Vernaccia
Gavi

Country Sausage Stew

Serves 4 to 6

Ingredients

- 1 pound kielbasa
- 1 medium onion, 1 cup chopped
- 1 teaspoon olive oil
- 2 carrots, 1 cup chopped
- 1 15-ounce can whole peeled tomatoes, stems removed and crushed (reserve 3 tablespoons of the tomato sauce from can)
- 1 48-ounce can chicken broth
- $\frac{1}{2}$ medium-size green cabbage
- $\frac{1}{2}$ teaspoon black pepper
- 1 tablespoon Pickapeppa Sauce
- $\frac{1}{2}$ pound spinach, chopped in large pieces
- 1 15-ounce can cannellini beans, drained (white kidney beans)

Directions

1. Cut kielbasa in 3/4-inch slices.

2. Sauté Kielbasa and onion in olive oil.

3. Add carrots, tomatoes, chicken broth, green cabbage, pepper, Picapeppa Sauce, spinach, and reserved tomato sauce; bring to a boil. After it boils lower heat to simmer and cook for 2 hours.

4. Add cannellini beans and simmer for 10 minutes longer.

Serve with French or Farm Bread.

Suggested Wine

Sangiovese
Red Zinfandel

Roast Duck with Raspberry Grand Marnier Sauce

Serves 4

Ingredients

2 ducks, fresh or frozen

2 carrots

1 onion

3 stalks of celery

Sauce

2 tablespoons granulated sugar

$1\frac{1}{2}$ cups raspberries, fresh or frozen

1 tablespoon Grand Marnier

1 cup chicken stock (reserve 1 tablespoon)

$\frac{1}{4}$ teaspoon arrowroot

Directions

1. Preheat oven to 450°.

2. Split ducks in half and rinse.

3. Dice carrots, onions, and celery and place in roasting pan.

4. Place the ducks on the bed of carrots, onions and celery, and bake at 450° for 10 minutes. Lower oven to 350° and bake for an additional 80 minutes or until the leg of the duck breaks away easily.

5. While ducks are cooking, melt the sugar in a heavy-bottomed pot until it is golden in color. Add raspberries, Grand Marnier, and 1 cup of stock, less 1 tablespoon. Reduce by a third.

6. Mix arrowroot with the reserved tablespoon of chicken stock and stir into raspberry mixture to thicken.

7. Purée sauce in a blender and pass it through a food mill using a fine grate.

8. Drizzle sauce decoratively on the plate and place duck on top. Serve with wild rice and fresh seasonal vegetables.

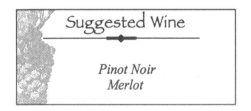

Suggested Wine

Pinot Noir
Merlot

Modified Chicken Marengo

Serves 4

Ingredients

2 pounds chicken pieces

$\frac{1}{4}$ cup oil

$\frac{1}{2}$ cup chopped onions

1 clove garlic, crushed

3 tablespoons flour

$\frac{2}{3}$ cup medium/dry wine

$1\frac{1}{4}$ cups chicken stock

1 tablespoon tomato paste

$\frac{1}{2}$ teaspoon salt

$\frac{1}{4}$ teaspoon pepper

1 cup mushroom tops

Chopped fresh parsley

Directions

1. Heat oil in large frying pan and fry chicken pieces until golden brown.

2. Add onions and garlic.

3. Stir in flour and cook for one minute.

4. Stir in wine, chicken stock, and tomato paste.

5. Add salt and pepper to taste.

6. Add mushrooms, cover pan and simmer gently for about 40 minutes.

7. Remove chicken to serving dish.

8. Reduce sauce by boiling if necessary.

9. Pour over chicken and garnish with parsley.

Serve on top of egg noodles.

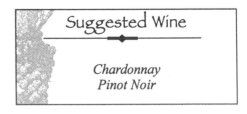

Suggested Wine

Chardonnay
Pinot Noir

Apple Cider Sorbet

You will need an ice cream maker for this wonderful sorbet that yields about a 1/2 gallon.

Ingredients

$\frac{1}{2}$ gallon apple cider

1$\frac{1}{2}$ cups sugar

$\frac{1}{2}$ cup of dark rum

1 teaspoon cinnamon

Juice of 2 lemons

$\frac{1}{8}$ teaspoon salt

* Fresh local cider makes the best-tasting sorbet.

Directions

1. Combine all ingredients in a bowl and whisk until sugar dissolves.

2. Process in ice cream maker until done.

3. Store in freezer for up to 2 weeks.

Pumpkin Sour Cream Custard Pie

Serves 8

Ingredients

9-inch pie shell

Filling

1 tablespoon milk

$\frac{1}{2}$ cup of sugar

18 ounces pumpkin purée (coarse)

1 cup sour cream

$\frac{1}{2}$ cup whipping cream

$\frac{1}{2}$ cup golden brown sugar

2 large eggs

1 teaspoon ground cinnamon

1 teaspoon ground nutmeg

$\frac{1}{4}$ teaspoon ground cloves

$\frac{1}{2}$ teaspoon salt

Topping

1 cup chilled whipping cream

$\frac{1}{3}$ cup of powdered sugar

Directions

1. Preheat oven to 350°.

2. Whisk pumpkin, sour cream, 1/2 cup of whipping cream, brown sugar, eggs, cinnamon, and all other spices in a large bowl.

3. Pour mixture into pie shell.

4. Bake in oven for about 35 to 40 minutes until set. Let cool, then refrigerate.

5. To make topping, whisk 1 cup of whipping cream and powdered sugar together until mixture peaks.

6. Serve chilled pie with topping.

Ginger Snaps

Makes 2 Dozen

Ingredients

$\frac{3}{4}$ cup shortening

1 cup white sugar

4 tablespoons molasses

1 egg

2 cups flour

2 teaspoons baking powder

1 teaspoon cinnamon

2 teaspoons ginger

Directions

1. Cream sugar and shortening.

2. Add molasses and egg and beat well.

3. Add dry ingredients and beat until smooth.

4. Refrigerate overnight.

5. Preheat oven to 375°.

6. Grease cookie sheet.

7. Form dough into teaspoon-size balls.

8. Roll in sugar.

9. Place 2 inches apart on cookie sheet.

10. Bake for 12 minutes.

Apple Walnut Supreme Cake

Serves 10 to 12

Ingredients

- 4 cups coarsely chopped, peeled apples
- 1¾ cups sugar
- 2 eggs
- ½ cup vegetable oil
- 2 teaspoons vanilla
- 2 cups sifted regular flour
- 2 teaspoons baking soda
- 1 teaspoon salt
- 2 teaspoons cinnamon
- ½ cup chopped walnuts

Directions

1. Preheat oven to 350°.

2. Combine apples and sugar; set aside.

3. In a large mixing bowl mix eggs, oil, and vanilla.

4. Beat one minute at medium speed.

5. Add combined dry ingredients, alternating with apple mixture.

6. Stir in walnuts.

7. Bake in a greased and floured 13 x 9x2-inch pan at 350° for 45 to 50 minutes, until cake tests done with a toothpick. Do not overbake.

8. If desired, drizzle top of cooled cake with Lemon Glaze.

Glaze:

Blend 1cup confectioners' sugar, 1 1/2 tablespoons lemon juice, 1/2 teaspoon vanilla, and 1 tablespoon corn syrup until smooth.

Ginger Pears

Serves 4

Ingredients

4 large pears

$1\frac{1}{2}$ cups heavy cream

$\frac{1}{4}$ cup superfine sugar

$\frac{1}{2}$ teaspoon vanilla

$\frac{1}{4}$ teaspoon cinnamon

Pinch of nutmeg

1 teaspoon grated fresh ginger

Directions

1. Preheat oven to 375°.

2. Cut pears in half; lay face up in dish.

3. Combine remaining ingredients.

4. Pour over pears.

5. Bake for 30 to 35 minutes.

Apple Brown Betty

Serves 8

Ingredients

Filling:

6 medium-size, Granny Smith apples, peeled, cored and cut into $\frac{1}{2}$-inch slices

5 tablespoons sugar

Topping:

1 cup all-purpose flour

1 cup light brown sugar

1 cup finely chopped pecans

1 teaspoon cinnamon

6 tablespoons unsalted butter, room temperature, cut into 6 pieces

Directions

1. Preheat oven to 350°.

2. Grease 8-inch square baking pan with butter.

3. Place one-half of the apples in the prepared pan and sprinkle with sugar.

4. Layer the remaining apples over the sugar.

5. Prepare the topping.

6. Place flour, brown sugar, pecans, and cinnamon in a large bowl and mix well.

7. Work the butter into the mixture until blended.

8. Spread the topping over the apples.

9. Bake 55 to 60 minutes or until topping is golden and apples are bubbling.

10. Serve hot with vanilla ice cream or heavy cream.

Pecan Pie Squares

Makes 20

Ingredients

Crust

3 cups flour

$\frac{1}{4}$ cup plus 2 tablespoons sugar

$\frac{3}{4}$ cup soft butter

$\frac{3}{4}$ teaspoon salt

Filling

4 eggs

$1\frac{1}{2}$ cups sugar

$1\frac{1}{2}$ cups light Karo syrup

3 tablespoons melted butter

$1\frac{1}{2}$ teaspoons vanilla

$2\frac{1}{2}$ cups chopped pecans

Directions

1. Preheat oven to 350°.

2. Combine the ingredients for crust in a food processor until well blended; press into the bottom of a lightly greased 15 1/2 x 10 1/2-inch pan and bake in preheated oven for 20 minutes.

3. Combine all filling ingredients in food processor and pour into pre-baked crust; return to oven for another 25 minutes. Cool in pan.

Energy Bars

Serves 10 to 12

Ingredients

$1\frac{1}{2}$ cups flour

$1\frac{1}{4}$ teaspoons baking soda

1 teaspoon salt

$1\frac{1}{2}$ teaspoons cinnamon

$\frac{1}{4}$ teaspoon nutmeg

$\frac{1}{8}$ teaspoon cloves

1 cup butter

1 cup brown sugar

$1\frac{1}{2}$ cups white sugar

1 tablespoon milk

$\frac{1}{2}$ teaspoon vanilla

2 eggs

1 cup crushed corn flakes

3 cups oatmeal

1 cup coconut

2 cups chocolate chips
(one 12-ounce package)

1 cup walnuts

Directions

1. Mix together first six dry ingredients.

2. In a separate bowl cream together butter, brown sugar, and sugar.

3. Add milk, vanilla, and eggs.

4. Stir in dry ingredients, then add corn flakes, oatmeal, coconut, chocolate chips, and walnuts.

5. Press into large sheet cake pan at 1/2-inch thickness and bake.

Poached Pears with Cognac

Serves 6

Ingredients

- 6 pears
- 1 pound berries (raspberries or whatever is in season, fresh preferred)
- 1 tablespoon of fresh lemon juice
- 1 teaspoon sugar
- $\frac{1}{4}$ cup of cognac or to taste

Directions

1. Peel pears, then slice off bottom so pears stand up.

2. Place pears in steamer pot with water on bottom; cover and steam for 20 minutes. This timing depends on the ripeness of the pears—if ripe use less steaming time.

3. Purée berries and put in saucepan.

4. Over low flame add lemon juice and sugar to the pureed berries; cook slowly for 3 minutes or until hot.

5. Add cognac and cook together for 2 minutes.

6. Place steamed pears on individual dessert plates.

7. Pour sauce over each pear and serve while hot.

Apple Cake

Serves 10 to 12

Ingredients

- 6 apples peeled, cored, sliced, or chopped
- 5 teaspoons cinnamon
- 5 tablespoons sugar
- 3 cups flour
- 2 cups sugar
- 3 teaspoons baking powder
- 1 teaspoon salt
- 1 cup oil
- 4 eggs
- $\frac{1}{4}$ cup orange juice
- 1 tablespoon vanilla

Great in the morning as well as for dessert.

Directions

1. Preheat oven to 375°.

2. Combine apple slices, cinnamon, and 5 tablespoons sugar in a small bowl to toss and coat apples. Set aside.

3. Combine the flour, 2 cups of sugar, baking powder, and salt in a large bowl.

4. Make a well in the center and pour in the oil, eggs, orange juice, and vanilla. Blend until smooth.

5. Spoon 1/3 of batter into greased deep angel food pan. (Batter will be very thick.)

6. Place 1/2 apple mixture around center. Try not to touch sides of pan.

7. Add 1/3 batter, followed by remaining 1/2 apple mixture then 1/3 batter.

8. If you have any apples left, place on top in decorative layer.

9. Bake at 375° for 1 hour.

10. Cool on rack completely before removing pan.

11. Serve with ice cream or by itself.

Cranberry-Pignolia Biscotti

Makes 2 Dozen

Ingredients

- ½ cup Pignolia nuts (pine nuts)
- ½ cup cranberries, dried and chopped
- ½ cup butter
- ¾ cup sugar
- 2 eggs
- 4 teaspoons grappa (may substitute vodka)
- 1 tablespoon of orange zest
- 1 teaspoon orange extract
- 2 cups flour
- 1½ teaspoons baking powder
- ¼ teaspoon salt

Easy and Delicious!

Directions

1. Preheat oven to 325°.

2. Toast the pignolia nuts carefully. Chop them by hand when cool enough to handle.

3. Cream the butter until fluffy and add the sugar; cream again until fluffy.

4. Beat in the eggs until the mixture is smooth.

5. Beat in the grappa, orange zest, and orange extract. Add nuts and cranberries.

6. Sift together the flour, baking powder, and salt and incorporate into the mixture only until just mixed (do not over mix).

7. Shape, with floured hands, into 2 logs.

8. Roll and bake for 25 to 30 minutes. Cool 5 minutes.

9. Slice on the diagonal.

10. Toast in oven 5 minutes on each side.

Date Nut Bread

Ingredients

1 cup chopped dates

1 cup chopped nuts

1 cup boiling water

1 teaspoon baking soda

1 cup sugar

2 eggs

2 tablespoons shortening

1 teaspoon vanilla

2 cups flour

$\frac{1}{2}$ teaspoon salt

Directions

1. Preheat oven to 325°.

2. Combine first 4 ingredients. Set aside to cool.

3. Cream sugar, eggs, and shortening. Add remaining ingredients and add cooled dates and nuts mixture.

4. Pour into loaf pan and bake for 35 to 45 minutes.

Cappuccino Chip Muffins

Makes 12 medium muffins

Ingredients

2½ cups unbleached all-purpose flour

½ cup sugar

2½ teaspoons baking powder

¼ teaspoon baking soda

½ teaspoon salt

½ cup semisweet chocolate chips

¾ cup brewed black coffee

½ cup (1 stick) unsalted butter, melted

¼ cup heavy cream

2 large eggs

1 teaspoon vanilla

Directions

1. Preheat oven to 400°.

2. Lightly butter 12 muffin cups; or coat with nonstick cooking spray; or use cup liners.

3. Combine flour, sugar, baking powder, baking soda, and salt in a large bowl.

4. Stir until thoroughly blended.

5. Stir in the chocolate chips.

6. In a separate bowl, whisk together the coffee, butter, cream, eggs, and vanilla.

7. Add to dry ingredients and fold together until evenly moistened. Do not over mix.

8. Divide batter evenly among the muffin cups.

9. Bake at 400° for 15 to 20 minutes.

10. Cool on a rack for 5 minutes before removing from pan.

Cranberry-Glazed Brie

Ingredients

1 wheel of Brie cheese
(8-inch diameter)

Apple slices

Pear slices

Crackers

Cranberry Marmalade

3 cups cranberries

$\frac{3}{4}$ cup packed brown sugar

$\frac{1}{3}$ cup dried currants

$\frac{1}{3}$ cup water

$\frac{1}{8}$ teaspoon dry mustard

$\frac{1}{8}$ teaspoons allspice

$\frac{1}{8}$ teaspoon cardamom

$\frac{1}{8}$ teaspoon ginger

Directions for Marmalade

1. Combine all in heavy non-aluminum saucepan and cook over medium heat until berries pop, stirring frequently, about 5 minutes.

2. Cool to room temperature.

3. Can be prepared up to 4 days ahead, covered and refrigerated.

Directions

1. Preheat oven to 350°.

2. Cut circle in top rind of cheese, leaving 1/2-inch border of rind, and carefully remove the circle of rind (do not cut through side of rind).

3. Place cheese in 8-inch diameter ovenproof serving dish.

4. Spread cranberry marmalade over top (can be prepared 6 hours ahead, covered and refrigerated, bring to room temperature before continuing).

5. Bake cheese until soft (approximately 12 minutes).

6. Set cheese on large platter, surrounded with crackers and fruit.

7. Serve warm or at room temperature.

Hot Crabmeat Dip

Ingredients

- 1 8-ounce package cream cheese
- 3 tablespoons mayonnaise
- 1 tablespoon lemon juice
- 1 teaspoon Dijon mustard
- 2 teaspoons horseradish
- $\frac{1}{2}$ teaspoon Worcestershire sauce
- $\frac{1}{2}$ pound Maryland crabmeat, drained
- Dash salt and pepper

Directions

1. Combine all ingredients well except crabmeat and cook slowly on low until smooth and hot.

2. Add crabmeat and blend well.

3. Serve warm with crackers.

Pears, Roasted Walnuts, and Gorgonzola Salad

Serves 4

Ingredients

2 pears

1 cup of walnuts, roasted

6 ounces of Gorgonzola cheese

2 tablespoons lemon juice

Mesculan salad mix

Directions

1. Peel and slice pears 1/8-inch thick and toss in lemon juice.

2. Arrange pears on greens.

3. Top with walnuts and crumbled cheese.

4. Serve with raspberry, champagne, or maple balsamic vinaigrette.

Persian Cucumber Salad

Serves 6

Ingredients

- $\frac{1}{4}$ cup walnuts
- $\frac{1}{4}$ cup raisins
- 6 medium garlic cloves
- 2 tablespoons olive oil
- $1\frac{1}{2}$ pounds seedless cucumbers
- 3 tablespoons minced mint
- $\frac{3}{4}$ cup plain yogurt
- Salt and pepper

Directions

1. Preheat oven to 350°.

2. Grind nuts in food processor and spread in shallow baking pan.

3. Toast until golden and fragrant, approximately 2 minutes. Cool.

4. Soak raisins in 1/2 cup hot water until plump, approximately 5 minutes.

5. Drain and reserve 1 tablespoon liquid.

6. Peel and mince garlic. Sauté in oil until soft, approximately 2 minutes.

7. Remove from heat and cool.

8. Peel, seed, and cut cucumbers into 1/2-inch dices.

9. Put all ingredients in medium bowl, including 1/2 teaspoon salt, 1/4 teaspoon pepper, and raisin liquid.

10. Toss and serve immediately.

Ched-Weiser Soup

Serves 4

Ingredients

4 tablespoons of butter

$\frac{1}{2}$ cup onions, diced

$\frac{1}{2}$ cup celery, diced

2 cloves garlic, minced

$\frac{1}{8}$ cup flour

1 cup chicken stock

1 cup milk

1 cup cream

8 ounces sharp cheddar cheese, shredded

1 bottle Budweiser beer

$\frac{1}{2}$ teaspoon salt

$\frac{1}{8}$ teaspoon pepper

$\frac{1}{2}$ teaspoon Hot English Mustard

1 tablespoon chives, chopped for garnish

Directions

1. In a 2-quart sauce pot, sauté onions, garlic, and celery with the butter.

2. Add flour and cook for a few minutes.

3. Add chicken stock, milk, cream and cheddar cheese; bring to simmer.

4. Add the beer and the seasonings and simmer for 20 minutes.

5. Sprinkle the soup with chopped chives.

Always save one glass of beer for the chef.

Lentil Soup

Serves 6

Ingredients

3 cups dry lentils (24 ounces, soaked overnight)

3 quarts water or vegetable stock

2 teaspoons salt

4-6 medium garlic cloves, crushed

1 cup chopped celery

2 cups chopped onions

1 cup sliced carrots

$\frac{1}{2}$ teaspoon dried basil

$\frac{1}{2}$ teaspoon dried oregano

$\frac{1}{2}$ teaspoon thyme

$\frac{1}{2}$ teaspoon freshly ground pepper

Directions

1. Place lentils, water or stock, and salt in soup pot and simmer, partially covered, for 25 to 30 minutes.

2. Add vegetables, herbs, and pepper.

3. Simmer another 20 to 30 minutes, stirring occasionally, until lentils are soft.

You can also use a slow cooker for 6 to 8 hours.

Note: This soup is fat free

White Bean Soup

Serves 4

Ingredients

$2\frac{1}{2}$ cups chicken stock

1 cup cooked white beans

$\frac{1}{4}$ cup onions, diced small

$\frac{1}{2}$ cup carrots, diced

$\frac{1}{2}$ cup celery, diced

$\frac{1}{2}$ teaspoon thyme, dry

1 bay leaf

White pepper to taste

1 bunch of fresh parsley, chopped

Directions

1. Boil beans in water until tender, following directions of package.

2. Strain and rinse with warm water.

3. Return to pot; add remaining ingredients, except parsley, and simmer 10 to 15 minutes over medium heat.

4. Heat four bowls in a 150° oven. Pour 3/4 cup soup into each and top with parsley just before serving.

Bouillabaisse

Serves 6

Ingredients

- $\frac{1}{4}$ cup dry white wine
- 1 medium onion, diced
- 1 clove garlic, minced
- 4 bay leaves
- $\frac{1}{2}$ pound tomatoes, peeled, seeded, and diced
- 1 cup celery, diced
- $\frac{1}{2}$ jalapeño pepper, diced
- $\frac{1}{8}$ teaspoon celery seed
- $\frac{1}{8}$ teaspoon ground white pepper
- 3 cups fish stock
- 2 tablespoons fresh tarragon, minced
- 2 tablespoons fresh parsley, minced
- $1\frac{1}{2}$ teaspoons Pernod Liqueur
- $\frac{3}{4}$ cup raw fish, diced (we recommend lowfat fish such as sole, grouper, snapper, or scallops)

Directions

1. Combine wine, onion, garlic, and bay leaves in a saucepan and cook over medium heat until reduced by half.

2. Add vegetables and pepper and simmer for 10 minutes.

3. Just before serving, add remaining ingredients and simmer until fish is cooked, approximately 5 minutes.

4. Heat six bowls in a 150° degree oven and pour 3/4 cup soup into each.

5. Garnish with parsley and tarragon.

Many Greens and Roasted Walnuts

Serves 6

Ingredients

- 2 cups kale
- 2 cups collards
- 2 cups mustard greens
- 2 cups red chard
- 1 cup walnut pieces
- 2 tablespoons extra-virgin olive oil
- 5 cloves minced garlic
- 3 tablespoons water
- 2 teaspoons tamari - shoyu

HINT - "Old kale" will remain tough no matter how long you cook it. How to define old kale? Either it's been in your refrigerator a week, or a few leaves are turning yellow. You can still use it, but use only the 3 to 4 inch tips of the stalks.

This is a "modified" stir fry: use just enough oil to coat the vegetables and a little bit of water and a lid to cook them tenderly without adding more oil.

Directions

1. Wash, pick over, and remove coarse stems of all greens. Cut greens into 3/4-inch wide pieces.

2. Roast walnut pieces in oven or iron skillet for 10 minutes.

3. Heat up Dutch oven or iron skillet. Add 2 tablespoons extra-virgin olive oil.

4. Add garlic and cook until fragrant.

5. Add greens (they will splatter if they are still wet from washing). Stir until all greens have been touched by the heat of the pan.

6. Add 3 tablespoons of water with 2 teaspoons of tamari and cover pot. Check in 2 minutes and stir.

7. Cover and check every minute. You want to cook the greens until tender, but you don't want the color of the greens to fade.

8. Remove lid to evaporate extra moisture for the last couple minutes before serving.

9. Greens are ready when they are reduced by about half, they are still vibrantly green, and the kale is slightly tender.

10. Serve tossed with the roasted walnut pieces.

Leafy Green Vegetables

Some vegetables provide more nutrition than others. Many fruits and vegetables are predominantly composed of water. Other vegetables are rich in vitamins, minerals, and trace elements. One half cup of parsley contains more Vitamin A and C than a whole head of iceberg lettuce. One cup of cooked collard greens contains 357 mg. of calcium compared to 291 mg. of calcium in one cup of milk.

When leafy, green vegetables are mentioned most people's minds turn to broccoli. Different ethnic groups utilize a variety of leafy green vegetables in their diets. No southerner would start the year without a bowl of collard greens and black-eyed peas. Mustard greens are another southern dish. The Portuguese have kale and sausage soup, and bok choy is an integral part of any Chinese feast. Don't forget watercress, arugula, brussel sprouts, cabbage, beet greens, young turnip greens, and parsley.

Many leafy green vegetables are extremely hardy and love growing in our Vermont gardens. After the first snowfall, kale sits like the sturdy soldier it is, still dark green and vibrant in the garden. Broccoli, collards, and spinach are also very hardy.

Spinach and chard are inferior to many of the leafy greens, because they contain oxalic acid. Oxalic acid is what leaves the tannic feeling in your mouth. It binds with minerals and carries them out of the body, making spinach and chard somewhat less beneficial than collards, kale, mustard, and bok choy. Don't stop eating them, but interchange them with other greens.

How you cook your leafy, green vegetables affects their nutritional content. Vitamin C and some of the B-complex vitamins are destroyed by high heat and boiling. All water-soluble vitamins dissipate quickly into the cooking water when you boil vegetables in a pot of water. Protein and minerals are sturdier and hold up well under cooking. You can avoid the loss of these much needed nutrients by steaming vegetables above, not in, water. Use your pressure cooker. Quickly stir-fry vegetables or eat young tender greens without cooking them.

— *Suzanne Smith, L.C.N.*

Corn Soufflé

Serves 6

Ingredients

- 1 cup frozen corn, thawed
- 2 tablespoons butter
- 2 tablespoons flour
- $\frac{1}{2}$ cup milk
- $\frac{1}{4}$ teaspoon salt
- $\frac{1}{8}$ teaspoon pepper
- 1 teaspoon sugar
- 3 egg yolks, beaten
- $\frac{1}{2}$ cup mushrooms, lightly sautéed
- 3 egg whites, beaten to soft peak
- 3 slices bacon, cooked crisp and crumbled
- Chopped parsley

Directions

1. Preheat oven to 350°
2. Melt butter in saucepan.
3. Add flour and stir until smooth.
4. Add milk and cook over moderate heat, stirring occasionally until thick and smooth, about 8 minutes.
5. Add corn, salt, pepper, and sugar.
6. Add a few tablespoons of the corn sauce to the beaten egg yolks, then add the yolk mixture back to the sauce, cooking over low heat for 1 minutes.
7. Remove from heat and add sautéed mushrooms.
8. Cool 5 to 10 minutes before adding beaten egg whites.
9. Place in buttered baking dish.
10. Bake for 35 to 40 minutes or until light brown.
11. Garnish with bacon and parsley.

North Country Potatoes

Serves 6 to 8

Ingredients

- 6 tablespoons butter, divided
- 2 cups shredded cheddar cheese
- 2 cups sour cream
- $\frac{1}{2}$ teaspoon salt
- $\frac{1}{4}$ teaspoon pepper
- $\frac{1}{2}$ medium onion, minced
- 6 medium potatoes, boiled in skins and refrigerated for 24 hours

Can be frozen, but completely defrost before cooking.

Directions

1. Preheat oven to 350°.
2. Melt 4 tablespoons of butter with cheese in a double boiler.
3. Add sour cream, salt, pepper, and onions; stir until well blended.
4. Remove from heat.
5. Peel potatoes and grate them into the cheese mixture.
6. Place mixture in buttered 2-quart casserole and dot with remaining butter.
7. Bake in 350° oven for 45 minutes.

Curry Sauce for Vegetables

Serves 6 to 8

Ingredients

- $\frac{1}{4}$ cup olive oil
- $\frac{1}{4}$ teaspoon cumin seeds
- $\frac{1}{4}$ stick of cinnamon
- 2-3 whole cloves
- 4-5 whole peppercorns
- 24 ounces (3 medium) onions, finely chopped
- 1 teaspoon fresh garlic, finely chopped
- 12 ounces (2 medium) tomatoes, skinned and chopped
- $\frac{1}{2}$ teaspoon ground red pepper
- $\frac{1}{4}$ teaspoon turmeric
- 1 tablespoon powdered coriander
- $\frac{1}{2}$ teaspoon salt

Directions

1. Heat olive oil and add cumin, cinnamon, cloves, and peppercorns.

2. Add onions and cook slowly until brown.

3. Add garlic and tomatoes and cook for 5 minutes.

4. Add remaining ingredients and cook until oil separates.

Stir in cooked vegetables such as potatoes, peas, eggplant, etc.

Can be frozen.

Spanish Potato Omelette

Serves 4

Ingredients

6-8 Yukon Gold potatoes, sliced thin

$\frac{1}{4}$ cup pure olive oil

8-9 eggs, room temperature

1 tablespoon butter

Salt and pepper to taste

$\frac{1}{4}$ cup chopped parsley or other fresh herbs, as desired

This might seem like a lot of kitchen calisthenics, but the finished product is well worth it, and its popularity will make you a pro in no time!

Grated cheese, small bits of smoked fish or meat, cooked leeks, onions or garlic also work well as garnishes for this omelette.

Potato omelettes work equally well for breakfast, lunch, snacks and even dinner.

Directions

1. Heat the olive oil in a large skillet.

2. Pat the potatoes dry and add to the hot oil in layers.

3. Flip to brown evenly on all sides.

4. While the potatoes are cooking, whisk the eggs in a bowl.

5. Add fresh chopped herbs, salt, and pepper to the egg mixture.

6. Add egg mixture to potatoes in the pan and shake to set a base for the omelette.

7. Reduce the heat and cook slowly, until the mixture is almost completely set.

8. Carefully place a plate over the top of the pan and invert.

9. Then slide the inverted omelette back into the pan to finish cooking.

10. Repeat the inversion process to remove the omelette and flip once more onto a serving plate.

Turkey Pot Pie

Serves 4 (dinner portions)

Ingredients

2 9-inch pie crusts

Sauce

3 cups chicken broth

1 cup heavy cream

8 tablespoons clarified butter

6 tablespoons flour

$\frac{1}{4}$ teaspoon hot sauce (Tabasco)

1 tablespoon lemon juice

Filling

4 cups chicken or turkey, cut into 1-inch pieces

6 tablespoons butter

$\frac{1}{4}$ cup chopped shallots

2 cups sliced carrots

$\frac{3}{4}$ pound sliced mushrooms

1 cup frozen peas

Directions

Sauce

1. Bring chicken broth and heavy cream to boil in large pan.

2. Reduce to 3 1/2 cups of liquid.

3. Add flour to clarified butter and blend.

4. Bring the broth and cream to boil again and add blended butter and flour, stirring with a whisk.

5. Then add hot sauce and lemon juice.

6. Continue to cook over medium heat for 5 minutes.

Filling

1. Heat 6 tablespoons of butter and add shallots.

2. Cook briefly.

3. Add carrots; cook 10 minutes.

4. Add mushrooms and cook 3 minutes longer.

5. Add poultry.

6. Run frozen peas under hot water for a few seconds and add to mixture.

Final Preparation

1. Preheat oven to 350°.

2. Blend all ingredients in sauce and pour into four (4) 12-ounce oven-proof dishes.

3. Cut pie crust a little larger than dishes, enough to overlap slightly.

4. Top each dish with pie crust. Cut steam hole in top of crust.

5. Bake in oven at 350° 30 minutes until golden brown.

Great use of left over turkey.

Old-Fashioned Vermont Beans

Serves 8 (dinner portions)

Ingredients

- 1 quart yellow eye beans
- $\frac{1}{2}$ pound salt pork
- $\frac{1}{2}$ teaspoon baking soda
- $\frac{1}{2}$ teaspoon salt (optional)
- $\frac{1}{2}$ teaspoon dry mustard
- 1 medium onion, peeled
- 1 cup or less Vermont maple syrup, depending on sweetness desired

Note: May also be cooked in slow-cooker.

Directions

1. Wash and pick over beans and cover with cold water.
2. Add soda and soak overnight.
3. Rinse and parboil in fresh water until skins wrinkle.
4. Drain off bean water and save.
5. Place whole onion in bottom of bean pot.
6. Add beans, syrup, and mustard.
7. Score pork and place on top of beans.
8. Add enough bean water to cover.
9. Cook at 325° for about 8 hours.
10. Check periodically and add bean water as needed.
11. Cook uncovered for last hour so pork will brown.

Wild Mushroom Shepherd's Pie

Serves 4

Ingredients

Stew

1 pound assorted wild mushrooms (chanterelles, morels, cepes, black trumpets, oyster, hen of the woods are all excellent)

2 medium carrots

2 medium onions

2 stalks celery

3 cloves garlic

2 bay leaves

3 sprigs fresh thyme

2 cups vegetable stock (chicken or beef broth will also work)

1 cup white wine

$\frac{1}{2}$ teaspoon salt

$\frac{1}{4}$ teaspoon black pepper

Oil for sauté

Potato Crust

6 large potatoes

1 medium onion

5 cloves garlic

6 tablespoons olive oil

Salt and white pepper

Coarsely chopped Italian parsley for garnish

Directions

1. Preheat oven to 375°.

2. Brush clean the mushrooms, washing with water only if the mushrooms are really gritty. Slice the larger mushrooms but try to leave the smaller mushrooms intact as much as possible.

3. Peel and chop the carrots, onions, celery, and garlic. Try to keep the sizing on the vegetables uniform.

4. In a large sauté pan or Dutch oven, add oil and slowly saute the vegetables until they are tender.

5. Add the mushrooms and toss gently for a few minutes.

6. Add the herbs, wine, stock, salt, and pepper; simmer until the liquid is reduced by half (about 20 minutes). Check seasonings and set aside.

7. Wash and peel the potatoes. Cut in small pieces and put in pot for crust; cover with cold water, add some salt, cover the pot, and boil until very tender, but not falling apart.

8. While the potatoes cook, peel and chop the onion and garlic; slowly sauté in 6 tablespoons olive oil.

9. When vegetables are very tender but not colored, pour garlic, onion, and oil mix into blender and blend until smooth, adding more olive oil if needed to get a smooth mixture.

10. When potatoes are cooked, drain well and allow to sit 1 to 2 minutes to "flower." Return to pot; add the onion-garlic purée and mash well. Season with salt and white pepper to taste.

11. In a casserole dish, pour in the mushroom mix. Cover the mix with potatoes either smoothing with a spoon or piping for a more formal appearance.

12. Bake until potatoes are browned and mushrooms are hot.

13. Garnish with parsley and serve.

This recipe may be made ahead and refrigerated.

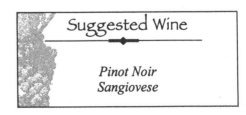

Suggested Wine

Pinot Noir
Sangiovese

Beef Wellington

Serves 4

Ingredients

4 6-ounce center-cut filet mignon (beef tenderloin)
2 ounces Foie Gras or goose liver pâté
1 sheet of frozen puff pastry (8x12)
1 egg

Mushroom Duxelle

6 large white mushrooms, chopped fine

1 teaspoon chopped shallot

1 tablespoon butter

3 ounces white wine

$\frac{1}{2}$ teaspoon salt

$\frac{1}{4}$ teaspoon pepper

Bordelaise Sauce

$\frac{3}{4}$ pint brown sauce (epangnol); beef broth may be substituted

8 ounces red wine

2 finely chopped shallots

$\frac{1}{2}$ teaspoon fresh thyme

$\frac{1}{2}$ teaspoon cracked black pepper

Arrowroot or Cornstarch as thickener

Directions

1. Preheat oven to 425°.
2. Season cuts of beef with salt and pepper; sear in very hot oil just enough to brown beef; do not cook meat past rare.
3. Place meat on a plate and cool.
4. Sauté mushrooms with chopped shallots in butter, for about 5 minutes; do not brown.
5. Add white wine, salt, and pepper and cook on low flame until dry.
6. Cut pastry into four squares and evenly spread pâté and duxelle in center of each pastry square; gently wrap pastry around meat so all edges meet at one point.
7. Flip beef over; beat egg with 2 tablespoons of water. Using a pastry brush, gently coat pastry with egg mixture.
8. Roast for 15 to 25 minutes. Using metal skewer or meat thermometer, check temperature in center of beef until 115° or very warm to touch.
9. Let rest for 5 minutes and serve on sauce.

Bordelaise Sauce Directions

1. Add red wine, shallots, pepper, and thyme to saucepan; bring to boil and reduce by half.
2. Add beef stock (brown sauce), return to boil, and thicken with arrowroot and water to desired consistency.

Suggested Wine

Cabernet Sauvignon
Red Bordeaux
Merlot

Grilled Salmon with Sundried Tomato Sauce

Serves 4

Ingredients

4 6-ounce filets of Atlantic salmon

Sauce

$\frac{1}{2}$ cup sundried tomatoes (not oil packed)

$\frac{1}{4}$ cup red wine

2 garlic cloves, sliced

1 shallot, sliced

$\frac{1}{4}$ teaspoon thyme

$\frac{1}{2}$ cup water

$\frac{1}{4}$ cup vegetable oil

$\frac{1}{4}$ teaspoon salt

$\frac{1}{8}$ teaspoon pepper

1 cup balsamic vinegar - to be reduced and drizzled over sauce

Salad

2 tablespoons extra-virgin olive oil

2 tablespoons fresh minced chives

3 tablespoons fresh lemon juice

$1\frac{1}{2}$ pounds fennel bulb, trimmed, halved, cored, and very thinly sliced

Directions

Sundried Tomato Sauce

1. In medium pot combine sundried tomatoes, red wine, garlic, shallots, thyme, and 1/2 cup of water. Bring to a boil over medium heat. Reduce the heat to low and simmer for 5 minutes.

2. Remove from heat and let stand, covered, for 20 minutes.

3. Transfer to a food processor and purée.

4. Add the vegetable oil in a slow, steady stream.

5. Scrape the sauce into a bowl and season with salt and pepper.

6. In a pot boil the balsamic vinegar over high heat until reduced to 1/4 cup, about 10 minutes.

The sundried tomato sauce and balsamic vinegar reduction can be cooled and refrigerated separately for up to 1 week.

Salad

1. In a large bowl combine 1 tablespoon olive oil with chives and lemon juice.

2. Add the fennel and toss well.

Salmon

1. Light a grill and brush salmon fillets on both sides with remaining 1 tablespoon olive oil and season with salt and pepper.

2. Grill over moderately high heat until nicely browned and just cooked through, about 4 minutes per side, depending on thickness of the fillets.

3. Spoon the fennel salad onto dinner plates and set salmon fillets on top.

4. Spoon the sundried tomato sauce around the fish and drizzle with the balsamic vinegar reduction.

Roasted Pork Loin with Three Mushroom Sauce

Serves 6

Ingredients

2-3 pound pork loin
4 garlic cloves, minced
2 tablespoons dried rosemary

Sauce

2 cups of water
1 ounce dried porcini mushrooms
2 tablespoons olive oil
6 ounces fresh portobello mushrooms, stems removed, caps sliced
6 ounces fresh shitake mushrooms, stems removed, caps sliced
6 tablespoons finely chopped shallots
$\frac{3}{4}$ cup cream sherry
$3\frac{1}{2}$ cups beef stock or canned broth
Salt and pepper to taste

Directions

Sauce

1. Combine 2 cups of water and porcini mushrooms in small saucepan, bring to boil. Remove from heat and let stand until the porcini are soft, about 30 minutes.

2. Heat oil in large skillet over medium-high heat, add portobello mushrooms, shitake mushrooms, and shallots and sauté until tender, about 5 minutes.

3. Add sherry and boil until most of the liquid evaporates, about 4 minutes.

4. Add beef stock, chopped porcini mushrooms, and reserved soaking liquid. Discard any sediment from the soaking liquid.

5. Boil until sauce thickens slightly and liquid is reduced by half, about 30 minutes. Season with salt and pepper.

Pork

1. Preheat oven to 425°.

2. Combine garlic and rosemary in small bowl.

3. Sprinkle pork with salt and pepper and rub garlic mixture over pork.

4. Place pork in roasting pan and roast for 10 minutes.

5. Reduce oven temperature to 350° and roast for approximately 25 minutes per pound or until meat thermometer registers 170°.

Bring sauce to simmer and stir in any pan juices from pork. Cut pork into slices, arrange on platter, spoon sauce over, and serve.

Suggested Wine

Pinot Noir
Sangiovese

Bulgarian Red Pepper Stew

Serves 6

Ingredients

- $\frac{1}{2}$ cup lentils
- $\frac{1}{2}$ cup navy pea beans
- $2\frac{1}{2}$ cups chopped onions
- 3 tablespoons vegetable oil or butter
- $2\frac{1}{2}$ cups seeded, chopped red peppers
- 2 teaspoons dried basil
- 1 teaspoon dried marjoram
- $\frac{1}{4}$ teaspoon dried thyme
- $\frac{1}{4}$ teaspoon cayenne
- $\frac{1}{2}$ teaspoon salt
- $\frac{1}{4}$ teaspoon pepper
- 3 cups vegetable broth or water
- $\frac{1}{4}$ cup dry red wine
- 2 tablespoons dry sherry
- $\frac{1}{4}$ cup tomato paste
- $\frac{1}{2}$ cup plain yogurt or sour cream
- Chopped parsley for garnish

Directions

1. Soak lentils and beans in water to cover for at least 4 hours.

2. Sauté onions until golden.

3. Add peppers and saute 5 minutes longer.

4. Add spices and sauté 1 to 2 minutes.

5. Add broth, wine, sherry, lentils, and beans and bring to boil.

6. Lower heat and simmer, covered, 1 1/2 hours.

7. Mix in tomato paste and cook several minutes longer.

8. If soup seems thick, add more broth or water.

9. Garnish with yogurt (or sour cream) and parsley.

Suggested Wine

Côtes du Rhône
Syrah

Black Bean and Sausage Chili

Serves 6

Ingredients

1 pound sweet Italian sausage

1 onion, chopped

2 cups beef broth

1 cup carrots, sliced

2 bay leaves

Chili pepper to taste

1 tablespoon vinegar

1 tablespoon dried oregano

1 tablespoon cumin

$1\frac{1}{2}$ cups corn

$\frac{1}{4}$ cup basil

2 cans black beans (19-ounce cans, drained)

Directions

1. Brown the sausage and onions, then drain.

2. Add rest of ingredients.

3. Simmer until carrots are tender.

Suggested Wine

Côtes du Rhône
Southern Italian reds such as
Salice Salentino or Ciro
California Rhône-style blends such as
Bonny Doon Big House Red

Grilled Free Range Chicken Breast with Braised Red Russian Kale and Vermont Mountain Cheese

Serves 4

Ingredients

- 4 boneless Bell and Evans chicken breasts or other free range chicken
- 1 medium onion
- 2 bunches red Russian kale
- Olive oil for sauté
- $\frac{1}{2}$ cup chicken broth
- $\frac{1}{2}$ teaspoon salt
- Pinch of black pepper
- 1 tablespoon malt vinegar
- $1\frac{1}{2}$ cups grated Vermont mountain cheese*

*excellent domestic Gruyere cheese

Directions

1. Preheat oven to 350°.

2. Split and trim the chicken breasts.

3. Pound them flat with a meat hammer or the bottom of a heavy skillet. Set aside.

4. Chop the onion. In a large saucepan with a cover, add the onion and sauté until soft.

5. Wash the kale. Take off the stems and tear into bite-size pieces.

6. Add the kale to the pot with the onion. Add broth, salt, pepper, and vinegar. Cover tightly and simmer until very tender (approximately 20 minutes).

7. Heat the grill. Grill the chicken breasts until almost cooked through (about 4 minutes per side).

8. Place kale mixture in a casserole, then lay chicken breast on top and cover with cheese.

9. Bake in hot oven until cheese melts and is lightly brown.

10. Serve at once with rice or buttered noodles.

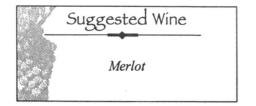

Suggested Wine

Merlot

Spaghetti with Eggplant Sauce

Serves 6

Ingredients

2 eggplants, peeled and chopped into $\frac{1}{2}$-inch cubes

2 tablespoons olive oil

4 garlic cloves, peeled and pressed through a garlic press

$\frac{1}{4}$ cup chopped parsley

$\frac{1}{4}$ cup chopped fresh basil leaves

$\frac{1}{4}$ teaspoon salt

$\frac{1}{8}$ teaspoon of pepper

2 cups of homemade tomato sauce

$\frac{3}{4}$ pound of fresh, whole milk mozzarella cheese, cut in $\frac{1}{2}$-inch cubes

$\frac{1}{4}$ cup grated parmesan cheese

Directions

1. Preheat oven to 350°.

2. Put diced eggplant on a greased cookie sheet and bake at 350° until soft. Set aside.

3. Heat 2 tablespoons olive oil in a large skillet over medium heat and cook the garlic, parsley, and basil until fragrant.

4. Add the eggplant carefully and cook 2 minutes until hot and lightly coated with oil and herbs. Season with salt and pepper.

5. Stir in tomato sauce and heat until mixture is hot.

6. Add the parmesan cheese and diced mozzarella and toss.

7. Serve over vermicelli or thin pasta.

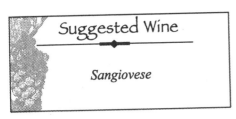

Suggested Wine

Sangiovese

Steak Diane

Serves 4

Ingredients

4 sirloin steaks, 6-ounces each, trimmed

$\frac{1}{4}$ teaspoon salt

$\frac{1}{8}$ teaspoon pepper

$1\frac{1}{2}$ ounces canola oil

1 tablespoon butter

1 tablespoon garlic

1 tablespoon shallots

4 ounces red wine

3 tablespoons Dijon mustard

2 ounces brandy

4 ounces heavy cream

4 ounces demi glaze

Directions

1. Season steaks with salt and pepper.

2. Pan sear on both sides in canola oil. Remove steaks and excess fat from pan.

3. Add garlic and shallots. Sauté in butter.

4. Deglaze with red wine.

5. Add remaining ingredients.

6. Simmer in sauce until steaks are done.

Curried Seafood Strudel with Shrimp and Crabmeat

Serves 8

Ingredients

- 1 sheet puff pastry, defrosted
- 4 tablespoons butter
- 2 tablespoons flour
- 1 cup of cream or milk
- 1 tablespoon fish bouillon
- $\frac{1}{2}$ teaspoon curry powder
- 12 ounces cooked crabmeat or lobster
- $\frac{1}{2}$ cup cooked orzo
- 1 tablespoon salt
- 8 medium shrimp, deveined, cooked, with tail left on
- 1 egg, beaten for eggwash (optional)

Directions

1. Preheat oven to 350°.

2. Melt the butter in a one-quart casserole.

3. Add the flour and cook over moderate heat for a few minutes.

4. Add the milk or cream until it thickens and becomes a smooth sauce.

5. Add the fish bouillon and curry powder. Remove from heat.

6. Fold in the seafood and the orzo. Adjust the seasoning and set aside.

7. Roll out the puff pastry sheet to approximately 12x16 inches. Place on a greased baking sheet. On each side of the 12-inch pastry sheet, make 20, 4-inch deep cuts. Make cuts along the 16-inch side about 1 inch apart, 4 inches deep.

8. Put the filling in the center of the pastry. Fold the strips over it, alternating from each side, until the strips are over the filling.

9. Egg wash the top. Bake at 350° until golden brown.

10. Cook the shrimp. Chill them. Place them with a toothpick at equal distances from each other in the center of the strudel.

Suggested Wine

Off-dry Riesling or Chenin Blanc

The orzo may be replaced by another grain such as cous cous or barley. The strudel may be served with a salad for a light dinner or lunch, or with a sauce or coulis as an appetizer.

Chicken Cutlets Matteo

Serves 4

Ingredients

1 pound chicken cutlets (boneless breasts, pounded thin)

Egg Batter:

2 eggs beaten together with $\frac{1}{4}$ cup of milk

Bread Crumb Mixture:

$1\frac{1}{2}$ cup Italian (or seasoned) bread crumbs

2 tablespoons fresh Italian (flatleaf) parsley

3 cloves of garlic, chopped fine

2–3 tablespoons fresh Locatelli Romano cheese, grated (or high-quality cheese)

$\frac{1}{4}$ teaspoon salt

$\frac{1}{8}$ teaspoon pepper

$\frac{1}{4}$ cup of olive or canola oil

1 pound mushrooms, sliced $\frac{1}{4}$-inch thick

1 small onion, chopped

$\frac{1}{3}$ cup chicken stock

Juice of $\frac{1}{2}$ lemon

Directions

1. Preheat oven to 350°.

2. Dip cutlets in egg batter, then in bread crumb mixture.

3. Sauté cutlets until golden brown on each side; set aside in baking dish.

4. Sauté mushrooms and onions together until onions are transparent and mushrooms are soft, but solid.

5. Add broth/stock, reduce 1 minute, and pour over chicken.

6. Bake in oven at 350 degrees, 15 to 20 minutes

7. Pour lemon juice over cutlets and turn off heat.

This dish can be prepared ahead up to baking point.

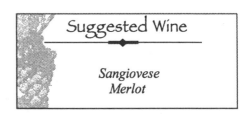

Suggested Wine

Sangiovese
Merlot

Hearty Vegetarian Winter Stew

Serves 6

Ingredients

3-4 potatoes peeled, and cut into small pieces

1 sweet potato, peeled and cut into small pieces

3 carrots peeled and sliced

3 shiitake mushrooms, stems removed and sliced

5 small onions, boiling variety

$\frac{1}{2}$ pound seitan, chopped

4 tablespoons olive oil

$\frac{1}{2}$ small onion chopped fine

2 cloves garlic, chopped

3 tablespoons nutritional yeast flakes

3 tablespoons unbleached white flour

2-3 tablespoons red wine

1 cup leafy greens, thinly sliced

3 stalks of celery, thinly sliced

1 tablespoon tamari

Suggested Wine

*Côtes du Rhône
Sangiovese*

Directions

1. In Dutch oven, steam potatoes, sweet potato, carrots, mushrooms, and boiling onions until barely tender. Save water and vegetables separately. Set aside.

2. In same Dutch oven, brown chopped seitan in olive oil. Set aside.

3. Use same pan to make a roux with 4 tablespoons olive oil, small chopped onion, and garlic. When onion is caramelized or browned, add 3 tablespoons nutritional yeast flakes and 3 tablespoons unbleached white flour.

4. Stir until browned.

5. Add red wine and stir until blended.

6. Add the saved vegetable cooking water to potatoes.

7. Add more water or broth to make 2 cups.

8. Add leafy greens and celery.

9. Add tamari and cook until thick.

10. Add seitan and cooked veggies.

11. Cover and simmer until greens and celery are tender.

Cranberry-Glazed Roast Pork

Serves 6

Ingredients

- 4 pounds boneless pork loin roast
- 2 teaspoons cornstarch
- $\frac{1}{4}$ teaspoon cinnamon
- $\frac{1}{4}$ teaspoon salt
- $\frac{1}{2}$ teaspoon grated orange peel
- 2 tablespoons orange juice
- 2 tablespoons dry sherry
- 1 16-ounce can (or 2 cups homemade) whole berry cranberry sauce

Directions

1. Preheat oven to 325°.

2. Combine all ingredients except pork in saucepan and cook over medium heat, stirring until thickened.

3. Place roast in shallow baking dish and roast for 45 minutes.

4. Spoon 1/2 cup glaze over roast.

5. Roast until internal temperature is between 155° and 160°, basting every 15 minutes.

6. Let stand 10 minutes before slicing.

7. Add dark drippings to reserved cranberry sauce mixture.

8. Garnish each slice of meat with glaze.

Arroz Con Pollo

Serves 6

Ingredients

- 6 boneless chicken breasts, cut in small pieces
- $\frac{1}{4}$ cup olive oil
- 1 large onion, chopped
- 1 green pepper, julienned
- 1 clove of garlic, minced
- 2 cups chicken broth
- 1 cup dry white wine
- 2 cups of white rice
- 1 pound of smoked turkey sausage, sliced in $\frac{1}{2}$-inch thick pieces
- 4 bay leaves
- 1 can chick peas, $15\frac{1}{2}$ ounces
- $\frac{1}{8}$ teaspoon of ground saffron
- 1 small jar of pimentos, 4 ounces
- 6 ounces of nicoise olives, pitted
- $\frac{1}{2}$ teaspoon salt
- $\frac{1}{4}$ teaspoon pepper

Directions

1. Heat olive oil in stock pot, add chicken. When chicken is brown remove from pot.

2. Add onions and stir until translucent, add green pepper and garlic; keep stirring, being careful not burn garlic.

3. Add chicken broth and wine and return the chicken to the pot and bring to boil.

4. Add bay leaves, salt, pepper, rice, sausage, and chick peas; stir all ingredients then reduce to a simmer.

5. Add saffron and stir, then add pimentos and olives. Cover pot and cook on low heat for 40 to 45 minutes.

6. Check after 30 minutes to make sure it is a consistent slow simmer. Remove bay leaves before serving.

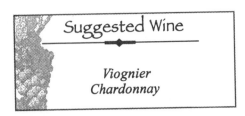

Suggested Wine

Viognier
Chardonnay

Jambalaya

Serves 6

Ingredients

1 large green pepper, cut into large chunks

1 large red pepper, cut into large chunks

1 large onion, cut into large chunks

3 stalks celery, cut into large chunks

2 tablespoons minced garlic

2 tablespoons olive oil

$\frac{1}{2}$ teaspoon Tabasco

1 tablespoon chicken base

$\frac{1}{4}$ teaspoon cayenne

1 teaspoon thyme

1 teaspoon oregano

$\frac{1}{2}$ cup fresh parsley

1 tablespoon Worcestershire sauce

3 pounds grilled andouille sausage (or shrimp, chicken or combination)

2 28-ounce cans diced tomatoes

Directions

1. Cook vegetables in olive oil until soft, approximately 5 minutes.

2. Add sausage, seasoning, and tomatoes. Simmer 30 minutes.

3. Serve over your favorite rice or pasta.

Very spicy!

Suggested Wine

Syrah
Red Zinfandel

Tuscan Stew

Serves 4

Ingredients

1 pound cannellini beans
(if dry, soak in water overnight;
if canned, drain excess juice)

2 tablespoons olive oil

1 onion, minced

2 cups chopped fresh tomatoes

$\frac{1}{4}$ cup fresh chopped basil

$\frac{1}{2}$ cup minced celery

$\frac{1}{2}$ cup minced carrots

2 ounces chopped prosciutto

Salt and pepper to taste

8 slices grilled country bread,
1-inch thick

Directions

1. Sauté onions, celery and carrots with extra virgin olive oil, basil, and prosciutto.

2. When vegetables are translucent, add tomatoes, salt and pepper. Simmer on low heat for 7 minutes.

3. Add beans and simmer 5 more minutes.

4. Serve over grilled bread.

Suggested Wine

Sangiovese
Red Zinfandel

Cheesecake

Serves 10 to 12

Ingredients

1½ cups graham cracker crumbs

¼ pound butter

¼ cup sugar

3 8-ounce packages of cream cheese

3 eggs

¾ teaspoon vanilla

¾ cup sugar

1 pint of sour cream

½ cup sugar

1 teaspoon vanilla

Directions

1. Preheat oven to 400°.

2. Blend graham cracker crumbs, butter, and 1/4 cup sugar together.

3. Press on bottom and halfway up side of springform pan.

4. Bake at 400° for 8 minutes.

5. Mix cream cheese, eggs, 3/4 teaspoon vanilla, 3/4 cup sugar. Beat until light and fluffy.

6. Blend in sour cream, 1/2 cup sugar, and 1 teaspoon vanilla.

7. Beat until smooth and pour into pan.

8. Bake at 400° for 1/2 hour.

9. Put under the broiler until light brown (watch carefully so that it doesn't burn).

10. Place on top of oven for 2 hours until set.

11. Then refrigerate.

Apple Cheese Torte

Serves 8

Ingredients

Crust

1 cup softened butter

$\frac{2}{3}$ cup sugar

$\frac{1}{2}$ teaspoon vanilla

2 cups flour

Filling

1 8-ounce package cream cheese

$\frac{1}{4}$ cup sugar

1 teaspoon vanilla

1 egg

6 apples, peeled and thinly sliced

$\frac{1}{3}$ cup sugar

1 teaspoon cinnamon

Fresh lemon juice

$\frac{1}{4}$ cup sliced almonds

Crust Directions

1. Cream butter and sugar.

2. Add flour and vanilla and blend well.

3. Press mixture into bottom and up sides of 9-inch springform pan.

Filling Directions

1. Preheat oven to 450°.

2. Beat cream cheese, sugar, vanilla, egg and pour into crust.

3. Toss sliced apples in bowl with sugar, cinnamon, and squeeze of fresh lemon juice.

4. Pour apple mixture over cheese mixture.

5. Sprinkle almonds on top.

6. Push crust down even with top of filling.

7. Reduce oven temperature to 400° and bake for 35 to 40 minutes.

8. Serve at room temperature.

Belgian Chocolate Pots

Serves 8

Ingredients

8 ounces bittersweet chocolate (good quality Belgian chocolates recommended)

3 ounces unsweetened chocolate

5 ounces butter

1 cup sugar

6 eggs

1 cup plus 4 teaspoon flour

$1\frac{1}{2}$ teaspoons baking powder

3 tablespoons cocoa powder

Directions

1. Melt chocolates and butter over double boiler.

2. Whisk in sugar and then eggs one at a time.

3. Sift in dry ingredients.

4. Butter 8 ovenproof ramekins.

5. Fill ramekins 3/4 full and chill. (May be stored covered in refrigerator up to three days.)

6. Preheat oven to 350°.

7. Bake at 350° for 10 minutes until risen and soft to touch (should be liquid in very center).

8. Serve with whipped cream and fresh berries.

Holiday Fruitcake

Makes 15 cups of batter

This fruitcake is made with dried fruits, not the traditional candied fruits.

Ingredients

1 16-ounce package of pitted prunes

1 8-ounce package of dried apricots, (1½ cups)

16 ounces of mixed dried fruit, (2 cups) we suggest pineapples, currants, papaya, cherries, cranberries, etc.

1 15 ounce package of raisins, (3 cups)

1 8-ounce package of pitted dates, (11/2 cups)

1 cup brandy

1½ cups of butter or margarine

2 cups packed brown sugar

6 eggs

3 cups all-purpose flour

2 teaspoons salt

1 tablespoon ground cinnamon

1 teaspoon ground nutmeg

1 teaspoon ground allspice

2 large ripe bananas, mashed

2 cups walnut halves

Cheesecloth

Directions

1. Cut prunes and apricots in fourths.

2. Dice the 2 cups of mixed dried fruit.

3. In a large bowl combine the prunes, apricots, mixed dried fruit, raisins and dates. Pour 1/2 cup of the brandy over the fruit. Cover and let stand 8 hours or overnight.

4. Preheat oven to 250°.

5. In large bowl, cream butter or margarine and brown sugar until fluffy.

6. Add eggs one at a time, beating well after each addition.

7. Stir together flour, salt, and spices. Add flour mixture alternately with the mashed banana to the butter mixture.

8. Stir nuts and fruit mixture into batter. Divide batter into well greased loaf pans. (Size of pans and baking times are listed below.)

9 x 5 x 3 inch pan . . . . 3 hours
• approximately 4 cups of batter

7½ x 3½ x 2 inch pan . . . . 2 hours
• approximately 3 cups of batter

4½ x 2½ x 1½ inch pan. . . . . . . 2 hours
• approximately 2 cups of batter

9. Bake in 250° oven for the time indicated or until golden.

10. Let cool in pans for 10 minutes; remove from pans and cool on a rack.

11. Pour remaining 1/2 cup of brandy over tops of cakes. Wrap in brandy-soaked cheesecloth and then in foil. Store in refrigerator.

12. Continue adding additional brandy to soak cakes occasionally.

This recipe can be doubled for additional cakes.

Chocolate Mexican Mousse

Serves 6

Ingredients

6 ounces semi-sweet chocolate

3 eggs, whites and yolks separated

$\frac{1}{2}$ pint heavy cream

3 tablespoons Kahluha

Directions

1. Over a double boiler, melt chocolate until smooth. Be careful not to overcook.

2. While chocolate is melting, whip egg whites until stiff peaks have formed.

3. In a separate bowl whip heavy cream until stiff.

4. Refrigerate both until ready to be added to melted chocolate.

5. When chocolate is melted, remove from heat.

6. Add the yolks one at a time to the chocolate using the Kahluha to moisten the mixture. Blend until all the yolks and Kahluha are incorporated into the chocolate.

7. Fold the chocolate mixture a little at a time into the egg whites.

8. Alternate layers of the whipped cream and chocolate mixture in a bowl.

9. Fold all together, keeping your action light, until thoroughly mixed.

10. Fill custard cups, wine glasses, etc. with the mousse.

11. Refrigerate for 3 to 4 hours or overnight before serving.

12. Garnish with shaved chocolate, whipped cream, or sliced strawberries.

Layered Chocolate Pâté

Serves 16

Ingredients

1st layer:

- 1 cup butter
- $\frac{1}{4}$ cup sugar
- 4 egg yolks
- 2 tablespoons Frangelico
- 2 teaspoons vanilla
- 8 ounces semi-sweet chocolate, melted
- 1 cup heavy cream, whipped

2nd layer:

- $\frac{1}{2}$ cup butter
- $\frac{1}{8}$ cup sugar
- 2 egg yolks
- 1 tablespoon Frangelico
- 1 teaspoon vanilla
- 4 ounces white chocolate, melted
- $\frac{1}{2}$ cup heavy cream, whipped

Sauce

- 2 cups fresh or frozen raspberries (thawed if frozen)
- $\frac{1}{2}$ cup confectioners' sugar
- 1 tablespoon fresh lemon juice

Directions

Make layers in separate bowls. Same directions.

1. Cream together butter and sugar.
2. Mix in egg yolks, one at a time.
3. Mix in Frangelico and vanilla.
4. Slowly stir in melted chocolate until smooth.
5. Fold in whipped cream thoroughly.
6. Line 2 loaf pans with Saran Wrap.
7. Spread 1/4 cup semi-sweet chocolate mixture in bottom of each.
8. Cover with half of white chocolate mixture.
9. Cover with remaining semi-sweet chocolate mixture.
10. Cover with Saran Wrap and chill at least 4 hours.
11. Purée the raspberries in a blender. Add in confectioners' sugar and lemon juice; blend until smooth. Strain the sauce to remove seeds.
12. Unwrap and serve, sliced, on raspberry sauce.

Chocolate with White Chocolate Chunk Cookies

Makes 4 dozen

Ingredients

- $\frac{1}{2}$ pound butter, unsalted at room temperature
- 1 cup light brown sugar
- 1 cup granulated sugar
- 2 teaspoons vanilla
- $\frac{3}{4}$ teaspoon salt
- $\frac{1}{2}$ cup plus 2 tablespoons cocoa powder
- 2 eggs
- 2 teaspoons baking soda
- 2 cups all-purpose flour
- $1\frac{1}{4}$ pound white chocolate, broken into small to medium chunks

Directions

1. Preheat oven to 325°.

2. Combine butter, brown sugar, and granulated sugar in a mixing bowl and beat until light and fluffy.

3. Add vanilla and salt and mix until blended.

4. Slowly add cocoa powder and mix until well blended.

5. Add eggs one at a time and blend well.

6. Combine flour and baking soda and add half of the dry mixture at a time.

7. Fold in chocolate chunks.

8. Scoop out a heaping tablespoon onto lightly greased cookie sheet.

9. Bake for 10 to 12 minutes until lightly golden.

Truffles—Shortbread Cookies

Makes 1 1/2 Dozen

Ingredients

- 3 sticks butter, softened
- 1 cup plus 2 tablespoons powdered sugar
- 3 cups flour, sifted
- $\frac{1}{2}$ teaspoon salt
- 1 teaspoon vanilla

Frosting

- 1 cup powdered sugar
- $\frac{1}{8}$ or less teaspoon vanilla
- Water

Directions

1. Preheat oven to 325°.
2. Cream butter and sugar together until light and fluffy.
3. Add vanilla and mix well.
4. Sift flour and salt together and add to creamed mixture; blend thoroughly. Cover and chill slightly.
5. Roll out chilled dough to 1/4-inch thickness on lightly floured surface and cut with cookie cutters of choice.
6. Transfer cut cookies onto ungreased cookie sheets and bake for 15 minutes or until just starting to color lightly (cookies should not brown).
7. Cool on rack.
8. Frost cookies when completely cool.

Chocolate Cream Pie

Serves 8

1 baked pie crust

Ingredients

$\frac{1}{2}$ cup sugar

$\frac{1}{3}$ cup cornstarch

$\frac{1}{2}$ teaspoon salt

3 cups milk

4 egg yolks, slightly beaten

2 ounces unsweetened chocolate

1 tablespoon plus 1 teaspoon vanilla

Directions

1. Stir sugar, cornstarch, and salt in saucepan.

2. Blend milk and eggs.

3. Stir into sugar mixture.

4. Cook over medium heat until the mixture thickens and comes to a boil. Boil for one minute.

5. Remove from heat; add melted chocolate and vanilla.

6. Pour into baked pie crust.

7. Refrigerate for 4 hours.

Desserts

ACKNOWLEDGEMENTS

We gratefully acknowledge all the restaurant owners, non restaurant-affiliated chefs and friends who were wonderfully generous with their recipes. We thank them all for the time and effort that went into their contributions: Jack Pickett, owner and chef of the Blue Moon Cafe; Elyse Moore of Food Vibrations; Diane McCarthy of McCarthy's Restaurant; Cabot Creamery of Cabot, Vermont; Barbara Hansel of Bittersweet Inn; Eve Lepcio of Stowe Coffee House; Kim and Doug Grant of the Lake Mansfield Trout Club; Lance Purnell of Catered Whims; Elizabeth Squire of Sage Sheep Farm; Paul Morris of Stowe Mountain Resort; Charlie Zimmerman of The Cliff House Restaurant; Kathy Kneale of The Depot Street Malt Shoppe; Audrey and Lew Coty of Nebraska Knoll Sugar Farm; the owners and chefs of Stowehof Inn, The Shed, Grey Fox Inn, Harvest Market, Green Mountain Inn, Trattoria La Festa, Partridge Inn, Olive's Bistro, Cactus Cafe, Gracie's, Sunset Grille, Olde England Inn, Brown Bag Deli, The Riverside Inn, The Gables Inn, Vermont Harvest, Stowaway and Topnotch at Stowe Resort and Spa; also Jacquie Talarico, Kitty Coppock, Deborah Beck, Ellen Thorndike, Will Buchan, Doreen Freeman, Maria Ayala, Jill Boardman and Ed Izzo, Maria Somweber, Becky McGovern, Judy Wagner, Janet Sedutto, Donna and Jake Carpenter, Julie Nitschke, Elaine Pinckney, Anu Ranawat, Adele Manning, Peggy Smith, Andi Pepper, Duncan Nash, Matthew Delos, Gunnell Clarke, Anne Steel, Jane Beatty, Louise Reed, Terri Sansom, Susie Fisher and Bob Rose, Sally Horwitz, Hubert Erhard, and Suzanne Smith, formerly of Food For Thought Natural Market.

Special thanks to Anton Flory and Roland Czekelius for their advice and guidance from the start of this project. Anton Flory was certified as a Master Chef in 1982 and started the New England Culinary Institute, one of America's outstanding institutions for up-and-coming chefs. Roland Czekelius was Director of the New England Culinary Institute when we first started this venture and is currently head of Food Services at Stowe Mountain Resort.

We extend our gratitude not only to all who contributed recipes, but to those who tested them, adjusted them, typed them, and proofread them! We extend our sincerest thanks to Rett Sturman, Paul Rogers, Nancy Cohn, Kathleen and Don Landwehrle, Tony Czaja, Elinor Earle, Mary Rocque, and Nanette McLane without whose talents and devoted efforts (more often on short notice!), the cookbook could not have been completed. Victoria Chapman, with your participation and moral support, *Vermont Tables in Season* is AT LAST a reality. Thank you.

— *Kathleen Buchan, Lynn Carrell, Paula Newman, Linda Post*

VERMONT
TABLES
IN SEASON

To order more copies of Vermont Tables in Season *please fill out and send in this form.*

Please send me Vermont Tables in Season
(ISBN 0-9663747-0-3)

Quantity:_____   @ $19.95   =   _____

Plus Shipping & Handling   =   _____
($1 per book)

                                 Total: =   _____

Please make check or money order payable to:

Friends of Our Schools Inc.
125 Deer Hill Lane
Stowe, VT   05672

Thank you and enjoy!